D0081493

World Debt and Stability

World Debt and Stability

George Macesich

New York
Westport, Connecticut
London

9-16-92

Library of Congress Cataloging-in-Publication Data

Macesich, George, 1927–
World debt and stability / George Macesich.
p. cm.
Includes bibliographical references.
ISBN 0-275-93669-4 (alk. paper)
1. Debts, External—Developing countries. 2. Economic stabilization—Developing countries. I. Title.
HJ8899.M32 1991
336.3'435'091724—dc20 90-37787

British Library Cataloguing-in-Publication Data is available.

Library of Congress Catalog Card Number: 90-37787
ISBN: 0-275-93669-4

First published in 1991

Praeger Publishers, One Madison Avenue, New York, NY 10010
An imprint of Greenwood Publishing Group, Inc.

Printed in the United States of America

The paper used in this book complies with the Permanent Paper Standard issued by the National Information Standards Organization (Z39.48–1984).

10 9 8 7 6 5 4 3 2 1

To the memory of

Walter Macesich, Sr.
1894–1975

and

Walter Macesich, Jr.
1928–1988

Contents

Preface

The heavily indebted developing countries appear hopelessly grounded. The high economic tide of the 1980s did not bring relief. As interest rates fell, interest payments in the leading fourteen debtor countries (the "Baker 15," excluding Yugoslavia) declined from a peak of 33 percent of their exports of goods and services in 1982 to 23 percent in 1987. In 1988, however, the ratio rebounded to 26 percent. This was despite a slight fall—the first in the 1980s—in the total debt of these countries, partly due to the increase in debt-equity swaps. Even with a boom in exports and a decline in the ratio of total debt to export earnings, the ratio of interest payments to exports was still almost double the figure at the start of the 1980s.

Creditor nations are offering some relief; some are converting loans to grants, while others are forgiving portions of the debt outright. In return, many debtor countries are adopting market-oriented economic reforms under strict structural adjustment programs funded by the World Bank and the International Monetary Fund. Thus far the discipline and the outside pressure have produced mixed results. To be sure, governments in many of the debtor countries must bear most of the responsibility for these results.

Bankers who provided the loans must likewise share in the responsibility. Indeed, in the closing months of 1989, a large international bank, J. P. Morgan and Company, increased reserves to 70 percent, from 23 percent, of its total loans to Third World debtor countries. This step was viewed as increasing the pressure on other international banks to do the same. The old loans to the debtor developing countries, of course, are not worthless, since the discount on them is not 100 percent. They vary in value from 18 cents on the dollar for Argentina to 50 cents on the dollar on loans made to Yugoslavia.

Creditor countries also come in for their share of criticism. Thus, the efforts of U.S. Treasury Secretary Nicholas F. Brady to reduce the international debt of the leading debtor countries has come in for sharp criticism, particularly by bankers.

They are concerned about debtor countries' rising expectations of the magnitude of debt reduction possible under the Brady initiative, when sufficient resources to encourage sizable voluntary debt reduction programs have not been provided by creditor countries. In their view, debt and debt-service reduction are not ends in themselves, and they certainly do not constitute an entitlement program. Bankers note the case of Venezuela, which has demanded a 50 percent cut in its foreign debt even though it has billions of dollars of gold and currency reserves and vast stores of oil. As a result, banks could be deterred from lending new money for economic development.

For their part, many economists hold that some developing countries are so encumbered by debt that their economic growth and social stability are threatened, so debt must be cut. In 1988, according to the World Bank's annual report, developing countries paid $50 billion more to creditors than they received in new aid.

In short, none of the participants in the world debt drama is without an explanation for the indifferent results produced by the vast international transfers of resources during the 1970s and 1980s. What to do now? This study puts forth the theory of cooperation as a useful framework with which to approach the world debt problem. There are, however, significant obstacles to cooperation in both creditor and debtor countries. These obstacles are discussed at length in the following chapters.

I am indebted to many people with whom I have discussed various aspects of the world debt problem. To Professors Marshall R. Colberg, Dimitrije Dimitrijevic, M. Cecil Mackey, Dragomir Vojnic, and Rikard Lang, I owe special thanks. My thanks to Mrs. Esther C. S. Glenn for assistance in preparing and editing the manuscript.

World Debt and Stability

1 World Debt

DEBT AND DEBTOR DEVELOPING COUNTRIES

The enormous foreign debt incurred by developing countries since 1973 threatens to seriously damage economic growth not only in the debtor countries but in the entire world economy as well. Aggressive steps must be taken to head off such a world disaster. There is not complete agreement, however, on what steps are to be taken and how they are to be implemented.

Most experts agree that much of the borrowing, especially by developing countries, has occurred to finance current consumption rather than investment. One consequence of such borrowing is that it does not generate income with which to defray interest and amortization charges, so that eventually future consumption must be sacrificed to meet these costs. Many countries have avoided these inevitable sacrifices by additional borrowing. The problems for these countries are thereby simply exacerbated. Eventually lines of credit are diminished, if not exhausted, and the country is forced to export more than it imports, using part of its export receipts to defray interest and amortization charges that were contracted in the past. As these resources are transferred abroad, the living standards in the country decline. Very likely the country will also restrict imports, with damaging effects on its economic growth as well as that of its trading partners.

The debt situation is particularly grave for small debtor countries. Their obligations are so great that they must pay annual interest and debt amortization to the extent that little foreign exchange is available to purchase essential imports. The consequent undermining of economic growth and reduced living standards in the several debtor countries also undermine social and political stability. The chain of events set in motion by these circumstances is now all too familiar: Import restrictions necessitate a combination of devaluation that produces adverse terms of trade, deflation whose immediate effect may produce unemployment, and exchange and trade restrictions that produce resource misallocations that further reduce real income levels. Import restrictions, when they reduce the import of capital goods, cast in doubt the country's ability to increase capital formation and employment.

The developed industrial countries also pay a price for developing country debt when their exports to debtor countries are curtailed as these countries restrict their imports. Moreover, the financial and banking stability in industrial countries is threatened as well. Large commercial banks in industrial countries are principal creditors for the debtor countries. A default by any major debtor country or countries could cause a severe financial and banking crisis. To be sure, it does not necessarily follow that a default that would impact on creditor banks would harm the economy at large. Deposit insurance and ability to control banks to provide the necessary liquidity by open market operations and direct lending to banks could protect the remainder of the economy. It would, of course, have very adverse effects on bank stockholders, who would indeed suffer losses. Whether governments should step in to bail out creditor banks for their follies in making uncollectible loans is a matter of debate.

Thus far major defaults have been avoided, although there have been suspensions of interest payments. It may well be tempting for a debtor country to default on its obligations. It is advised that it put aside any such temptation. The country doing so will very likely eliminate any prospect for obtaining credit in the future. Developing countries do need financing for the capital goods produced in industrial countries that embody new technology and for other imports if they are to develop. Credit lines very likely would not be forthcoming to a defaulting country.

Circumstances that brought both developed and developing countries the debt problem are now clear. The huge increase in debt between 1973 and 1978 coincided with the first Organization of Petroleum Exporting Countries (OPEC) oil price increase. The further doubling of oil prices in 1979 added the second debt explosion. The third big increase came during the worldwide recession of 1982–83. The debt grew from $130 billion in 1973 to $686 billion in 1983 to $1.3 trillion in 1989. A ranking of the leading world debtor countries is presented in Table 1.1.

Blame for the creation of the debt problem has been attributed to OPEC for raising the price of oil, to bankers for making uncollectible loans, and to high interest rates and sluggish growth in industrial countries. Many countries, nevertheless, managed to come through these disturbances without major debt increases. For instance, Asian countries even managed to improve their economic situations during the 1970s and 1980s. The bulk of the debt explosion occurred in Latin America, Africa, and some European countries. Indeed, the United States itself has become the world's largest debtor as a result of the country's cumulative current account deficits of the 1980s. According to some observers, the common characteristics shared by the United States and such international debtors as Latin American countries were the maintenance of overvalued exchange rates for too long and the use of international credit to finance domestic consumption at the expense of investment. The similarity between the United States and other debtor countries is probably overdrawn. Unlike the developing debtor countries, the United States continues to be an attractive country in which to invest.

CHARACTERISTICS OF SUCCESSFUL ADJUSTMENT

Why were some countries more successful than others in dealing with debt-associated problems? Several reasons come readily to mind.[1] These include the role prices, including interest rates and markets, play in the economy; stability in the monetary environment, including product management of the stock of money; an outward-oriented growth strategy; a favorable exchange rate policy; and, some would add, realistic exchange controls.

Our theory and experience suggest that prices, including interest rates, should reflect actual market conditions. They do not always do so. In

Table 1.1
Ranking the World's Debtors (by external debt to public and private entities)

Country	Total Debt 1988 (in billions of U.S. dollars)	Per Capita GNP 1987 (in U.S. dollars)	Ratio of Debt to Exports (in percent)
Brazil	$120.0	$2,020	26.7
Mexico	107.0	1,820	30.1
Argentina	60.0	2,370	45.3
Venezuela	35.0	3,230	22.4
Nigeria	31.0	370	10.0
Philippines	30.0	590	22.7
Yugoslavia	22.0	2,480	13.3
Morocco	22.0	620	23.4
Chile	21.0	1,310	21.1
Peru	19.0	1,430	12.5
Colombia	17.2	1,220	30.7
Cote d'Ivoire	14.2	750	19.6
Ecuador	11.0	1,040	20.7
Bolivia	5.7	570	22.1
Costa Rica	4.8	1,590	12.1
Jamaica	4.5	960	25.8
Uruguay	4.5	2,180	24.4

Source: *New York Times* (March 11, 1989), p. 19.

good part, governments use the interest rate and other prices as a tool in their attempts to stimulate economic growth. Such manipulation of prices is not very successful, to judge from the record.

In its sixth World Development Report, the World Bank examines the way developing countries control prices, including interest rates, exchange rates, and wages, as well as many others.[2] In one sample of developing countries, the World Bank finds that prices in the 1970s were controlled least in Malawi and most in Ghana, with a wide range in between. The bank used its index of price distortions to estimate what each country's growth was and then compared that estimate with what actually happened. The evidence shows that growth depends on many things, for example, resources and political stability apart from price distortion. Nevertheless, price distortion could explain about one-third of the variation in growth among countries. As the bank succinctly puts it, "prices do matter for growth."

The more farsighted governments should and do take such evidence seriously. They understand that entrepreneurial skill and human capital, rather than politicians and bureaucrats, are the mainsprings of development. Moreover, it is extremely difficult to dismantle official controls over the direction of credit and investment once they are established.

Even so, no developed country has found that merely establishing the appropriate financial framework—proper supervision, prudent lending, ensuring the absence of fraud—is the end of its task. For instance, governments will not allow foreign banks to establish themselves within domestic banking systems and give them free rein there. Few local banks, so the argument goes, would be able to compete. Every country feels the need for a home-grown financial sector, because of the central role banks play in economic and monetary policy.

Most developing countries share another characteristic. They all fail to cast the commercial banking net wide enough. Artisans and farmers, who typically comprise between 50 and 80 percent of the total labor force, rely on family, friends, or money lenders for credit. Such lending institutions as the government typically favor larger economic units. Subsidized credit, moreover, means rationing the amount available, usually at the expense of smaller operators.

Developing countries also share a lack of confidence in financial institutions, which results in weak banks and weakening confidence in proper assets, generally making it difficult for a long-term capital market to develop. Gold holdings in many of these countries underscore the lack of confidence in financial institutions. Several of these countries need to widen their financial markets to get more people to hold bank money. They also need to deepen their capital markets so that institutions can give better service to individual companies' financial needs.

Failure to allow the market to play its role almost assures that money and the monetary system will not be allowed to play a nondiscriminatory and autonomous role within the constraints of a rules-based policy system so necessary to ensure the preservation of economic and monetary stability in the country. It assures that money will slip into the political arena and become a political issue. Its manipulation to pursue changing goals and objectives will make money capricious, subject to varying political objectives, and incompatible with a stable monetary order. Monetary manipulation thus assures the instability and inflation so characteristic of emerging and debtor nations.

There are important external constraints to national sovereignty that place limits on money and monetary policy in these nations. In effect, the evidence suggests that the money supply in these countries grows at a rate that over the long run maintains an equilibrium in the foreign balance. Monetary authorities cannot influence excess money stock unless they are also willing to change the exchange rate.

This is consistent with the monetarist or quantity theory of money position on the importance of so structuring the monetary system that it will not fall prey to manipulation for political purposes. It underscores that money and the monetary system must be allowed to play a nondiscriminatory, autonomous role within the constraints of a rules-based policy system. At the same time, such a policy system of rules will serve to constrain the bureaucracy, the elite, and other interests from the use of monetary manipulation to serve their immediate interests.

The money printing and manipulating monopoly of the nation-state is the heart of the bureaucratic system. Given the records of many emerging Third World countries and others, a printing press can be very dangerous. These countries can either use some stable currency or constrain their bureaucracies within a lawful rules-based system.

IMPORTANCE OF EXPORT-ORIENTED STRATEGY

Consider, first, growth strategy implemented by the several countries under review. Countries experiencing the greatest debt problems focused their growth strategy on import substitution as against export promotion. Essentially such a strategy attempts to develop domestic industries that produce goods to displace imports—thus reducing dependence on imports and exposure to foreign shocks. The strategy promotes so-called infant industries in the form of tariffs, quotas, and subsidies. Even when well managed, such industries are inefficient. They cannot compete on the international market. Since their market size is limited to the domestic market, they usually cannot enjoy economies of scale available to firms participating in the larger international market.

The strategy of import substitution violates a basic premise put forth by Adam Smith in his classic *Wealth of Nations*. It is better, advised Smith, to promote exports, because success in foreign markets requires efficient production, favorable relative prices, and competent managers capable of carrying out the tasks at hand. There is also a tendency for a country adopting an export strategy to opt for an undervalued currency. As a consequence, its import demands will tend to be more modest than otherwise so that the country will be able to finance such imports from the proceeds of the exports without acquiring a large foreign debt. But now, if the country does resort to foreign borrowing, it may do so in relative comfort because of its export expansion, which will hold its debt-export ratio to reasonable levels. It will also enjoy large gains in labor productivity because of the economies of scale provided by a larger foreign market. In effect, such Asian countries as Japan, South Korea, and Taiwan are but more recent examples of Adam Smith's argument that the division of labor is limited only by the size of the market.

Of course, a country is not likely to succeed in carrying out an export-oriented strategy if its currency is overvalued with respect to the rest of the world's currencies. An overvalued currency makes it difficult for a country to export; it encourages imports, and current account deficits are the likely result. These deficits are then typically financed by borrowing abroad. Many Latin American countries whose currencies were overvalued as judged by purchasing power/parity criteria during the 1970s and early 1980s are a case in point.

There are positive aspects to an overvalued currency. In the very short run, domestic consumers enjoy goods and services, including travel abroad, that are inexpensive in terms of domestic currency. Some observers would place the United States in such a category for the period 1980–85, when high U.S. interest rates attracted foreign capital, which enabled the country to finance a current account deficit.

Not all countries had such an option. Latin American countries, as well as others, financed their current account deficits by borrowing from commercial banks. For example, Mexico, an oil producer, was unwilling or unable to take corrective action when oil prices broke and undercut the high value of its currency. It resorted to heavy borrowing abroad and became the second largest Latin American debtor, as its debt rose from $8.6 billion in 1973 to $82 billion in 1982.

Conditions in a number of countries are also further complicated by inappropriate and counterproductive exchange controls. Asian countries, for instance, managed to conserve foreign exchange by holding down "nonessential" imports. Many Latin American countries, on the other hand, were unable to do so, with the result that their current account deficits grew rapidly. Argentina, Mexico, and Venezuela come readily to mind as examples of countries where massive capital flights occurred, further increasing their debt problems.

A ROLE FOR CREDITOR COUNTRIES

To judge from recent reports, creditor countries are urged to make economic adjustments and growth in debtor countries more immediately politically palatable to those countries.[3] According to the International Monetary Fund (IMF), some developing debtor countries burdened with debt and faced with calls from creditors for economic reform expect to gain "limited short-term domestic benefits" from such reforms and, therefore, lack the necessary incentives to pursue them. The net effect may well be to undermine political support for policies that in the longer run would clearly improve welfare in the debtor countries.

Little support is to be found in such organizations as the IMF for debt forgiveness as an alternative to a comprehensive and workable plan to reduce world debt. In their view, global schemes for general debt forgiveness would not address the specific problems of individual countries. Moreover, such schemes typically carry serious difficulties in design, finance, and moral hazards. Furthermore, it is unlikely that these schemes would provide appropriate incentives for policy adjustments. In their view, the best approach for debt relief is on a case-by-case basis between official creditors and individual debtor countries. They argue that the private sector could do more to support growth in those countries that are undertaking adjustment programs.

Creditor countries could also do more to encourage creditors to assist in the readjustment process in debtor countries by allowing for greater flexibility in accounting and banking regulations when renegotiations of loan terms take place. In addition, a more comprehensive framework for negotiations between debtors and creditors could encourage the two sides to work more effectively to better realize the growth potential of debtor countries and thus improve their creditworthiness.

A satisfactory solution would require that world banks play an important role because of their unique characteristics. For instance, large world banks, unlike many of the smaller banks, have a long-standing relationship with a given country that enables them to take a longer-term view when dealing with their foreign clients. They tend to have less incentive to declare a default on loans. Many of these foreign loans are unsecured foreign government loans or are guaranteed by a foreign government. As a result, debt servicing may be interrupted, but most, although not necessarily all, loans are eventually repaid.[4]

Various proposals put forward as possible solutions to the debt problem include massive refunding operations, mandatory transfer of bank claims to new international organizations, and systematic stretching out of existing maturities. Important support would also include a more automatic supply of short-term liquidity by the Bank for International Settlements (BIS) and the IMF, and the creation of a market for bank claims with some official support by central banks. A system of partial guarantees by uni- or multilateral world institutions, not national governments, to help commercial banks make new loan commitments and adequate surveillance by the IMF to ensure that new lending will support sound economic policies are also methods that would work toward assisting developing debtor countries.

This does not mean that developing debtor nations will be relieved from dealing with long-run problems related to the structural aspects of the debt crisis—essential problems with great social implications and effects on employment and population, natural resources and energy, innovation, and capital formation. Similar structural problems face many of the developed creditor countries as well. If developed creditor nations are able to maintain monetary stability and avoid inflation, forgoing protectionist measures and keeping the debt issue in the proper perspective as an opportunity to promote global cooperation, the world will be the better for it.

Can there be a satisfactory resolution to the debt issue in a world in which debtor and creditor countries have diverse socioeconomic and political systems based on different ideologies and different levels of development? The solution will certainly require diplomacy—the process of eliminating or reducing conflict through reflection, talk, and bargaining—which is now more valuable than ever in dealing with the global debt issue. Diplomacy permits—demands, if one is serious—genuine exchange of views. Diplomacy allows one to find out the other country's needs, which may turn out to be compatible with one's own. Diplomacy's give-and-take tests the importance of one's own country's needs. Successful diplomacy leaves in its wake good relations, mutual trust, and hope for better times. It is not a failure of will for developed creditor countries to listen to the proposals of those countries that are weaker or even hostile. We usually honor that quality when we see it in private life. Moreover, the debt issue and the growing fear of protectionism have already changed the terms of the dialogue with the strong.

Some accords are imperfect, which is generally the nature of compromise and human affairs. Some have been a matter of luck rather than skillful achievements—such is a happy contingency of diplomacy. Some happened because a country was ready to retaliate in kind—such retaliation is a useful reserve, as we shall see, for those occasions when the other party insists on a course of action irrespective of the consequences for anyone else.

MARKET-ORIENTED DEBT REDUCTION

Market-oriented debt reduction approaches have increasingly attracted the attention of both creditor and debtor countries. The growing popularity of such approaches is the recognition that debtor countries are unlikely to repay in full on their contractual obligations. The evidence abounds in the growing secondary market, where the obligations of many debtor countries are traded in large and growing discounts. The secondary debt market has grown from a 1987 cumulative total of $6 billion to $8 billion to a range of $15 billion to $20 billion in 1988, or about 5 percent to 7 percent of outstanding Latin American debt.[5]

The rapid development in the secondary debt market can be attributed to two factors. First, during the 1980s, many regional commercial banks for which the Latin American debt is only a relatively small fraction of their assets or capital made sufficient loss provisions and were willing to cut their losses and get out. The second reason is that many debtor countries have made it easier for banks to move out by offering schemes that allow them to capture some of the discount. These approaches or techniques are now called "market-oriented," because they rely to some extent on market value of debt.

One widely used technique is that of debt-for-equity swaps. The basic idea is that a prospective foreign investor buys a country's debt at the market discount from the original creditor. The purchaser then exchanges the foreign debt at the central bank for local currency either at its face value or more likely at a discount somewhere between the face value and the discounted price. The local currency is then used to finance local equity participation. In effect, the operation gives the foreigner a preferential exchange rate. For its part, the debtor country reduces its external debt by the full face value, forgoes future interest payments, and may also appropriate part of the discount. Critics of debt-for-equity swaps argue that efforts simply serve to grant a subsidy to foreign investors who would, presumably, have sought equity participation with foreign currency in any event. They also point to the danger of excessive money creation in countries already infected with high inflation. To these perceived shortcomings of debt-for-equity swaps may be added the nationalist concern that such measures simply serve to turn the country's economy over to foreigners.

A more direct means for carrying debt-for-equity swaps is a simple straight buy-back by debtors, assuming that they have access to foreign exchange. For example, private firms in Mexico have reduced their foreign debt by more than half by offering to buy back their debt at a discount with appropriate foreign exchange funds. These matters are relatively simple to carry out in the private sector because of the limited number of creditors and debtors involved, so that agreements on the discount rate are more readily reached. Much more complicated are the buy-backs of sovereign debt incurred with bank syndicates. A major difficulty with such an approach is to get all syndicated creditors to agree to changes in the terms of loans in order to allow the buy-back. A modified version of debt buy-backs is for the debtor to swap old debts at a discount with its creditors for long-term fixed-rate (or exit) bonds. A major advantage of this approach is that since it is not a cash operation, agreement from all bank creditors is not necessary under the standard conditions of syndicated loans.

Another method is the so-called debt-for-trade swaps between indebted countries. Thus, about 40 percent of the trade of developing countries takes place among themselves, thereby providing an opportunity to use debt-for-trade swaps. Still another method advanced by academicians is debt-for-development, whereby a portion of the country's debt could be used to promote university research and development as well as investment in the human agent, which in many debtor countries is all too often a major obstacle to development.

Yet another option for creditors to choose in negotiating with debtors would link former U.S. Secretary of the Treasury Baker's plan and U.S. Secretary of the Treasury Brady's plan to exports. This proposal, advanced by a prominent French banker and an Argentine financial expert, would create a guarantee fund that would ensure future delivery of debtor country exports.[6] Accordingly, the $20 billion made available by the IMF and the World Bank in response to the debt relief plan put forward in March 1989 by Secretary Brady would be used to guarantee contracts for delivery worth up to $400 billion of debtor country commodities.

The delivery guarantees would presumably enable debtor countries to enter into long-term contracts to sell part of their future commodity exports. These contracts would then serve as collateral to borrow fresh money from the banks. That money would be used to buy back the debt at a discount.

Estimates made by investment bankers suggest that by entering a ten-year contract for 20 percent of its annual exports, Venezuela could obtain approximately $13 billion—an amount that would significantly reduce its $24 billion debt outstanding in 1989. A similar estimate for Brazil would give it $18.5 billion with which to reduce its $61 billion commercial debt.

The private French banker's proposal emphasizes that the official funds used as a delivery guarantee pool could make available money to be used for debt reduction that far exceeded the $20 billion that international institutions in 1989 were willing to lend for that purpose. Moreover, under the plan in place in 1989, the $20 billion to finance debt relief would just be added onto the debt burden of borrowing countries. The proposed plan provides that money borrowed against future exports would be self-liquidating upon delivery of the goods. Furthermore, the proposal does not represent a mortgage of the national heritage. This has already occurred the moment the government signed the initial contracts. The plan of profiting from the discount on the debt purchased enhances the value of exports that normally would have been used to prepay the full value of the debt. Export credit agencies in the industrial countries agreed to participate in financing future national imports at a level much more than the $20 billion in official funds that could become available.

The most likely exports from debtor countries that would be financed under such a scheme are commodities for which a large international market exists, in fairly standardized varieties and at prices that are quoted regularly on at least one organized exchange—on such commodities as oil, iron ore, copper, sugar, cocoa, cotton, coffee, and corn, as well as meat and fish products. The actual price paid would be the price at the time of delivery. Revenue shortfalls occur if the delivery price used to value the contract could be made up by either higher delivery amounts or an extended delivery period.

The incentives for importers to set up such long-term supply agreements are provided if the settlement price is at an agreed-upon discount from the spot price. Commercial banks could leave an incentive in lending new money, since the loans would be collateralized by the guarantee fund. The risk assumed by the banks discounting the sales agreements would be not that of the exporter but that of the purchaser, or of the guarantor in case of nondelivery, according to the proponents of the proposed plan. To ensure that the export proceeds are used to retire existing debt, the payments could be made to a trustee under irrevocable instructions to disburse the money only for repurchasing debt. Since the products would have to be exported, delivery defaults would be rare, and it would be easy and inexpensive to extend such guarantees.

WHERE TO NOW?

The principle of debt reduction in the Brady plan has much to recommend it even though debt relief does have its problems. Bad loans, however, are the fault of both borrower and lender. When countries that should be experiencing a new inflow of capital to finance development are instead exporting it, the situation is indeed critical.

The banks are in no hurry to be forthcoming to their debtors. They are receiving interest. They have managed, for the most part, to build up substantial reserves against potential losses. They say their obligations to shareholders require a hard line. A bank is not a philanthropy even where there might be compelling reasons for generosity. It must try to conserve assets. Nonetheless, there is the suspicion that banks see some of the debtor countries as of strategic importance to the United States and thus have a bargaining point to influence the U.S. government to step in and bail them out of their mistakes with such guarantees as the World Bank or others may provide.

A plausible lever to encourage banks to be more understanding of the plight of their customers may well be Article VIII, Section 2(b) of the IMF Articles of Agreement. This allows member countries to write exchange controls rules that make "exchange contracts" unenforceable in other countries. Whether loan agreements are exchange contracts is subject to legal challenge, but it is possible to envision paying some debts in the currency of the debtor country rather than in dollars. If a debtor country successfully invoked this clause, it could pick and choose which debts it wished to honor fully, thereby applying significant pressure to individual banks.

Application of Article VIII, Section 2(b) might indeed focus the attention of bankers on the needs of their debtors. It would also, unfortunately, involve the use and extension of exchange controls—not a promising prospect for those of us who are not favorably disposed to such controls. Still, it would be a way to provide bargaining leverage to debtors and then facilitate the settlement of the debt crisis, which is disruptive to international trade and the internal offices of both creditors and debtors.

The Brady proposal is an important departure from most of the decade of the 1980s, which emphasized continued new lending by the banks and international financial institutions. The Brady proposal's cornerstone is a $30 billion plan to restructure the debtor country debt. But its requirement that commercial banks subscribe $20 billion of that in new credits has proved a problem.

Various means and devices for attacking the world debt problem are being cast forth for consideration. Unrecoverable debts are being reduced, swapped for other assets, or even given away by banks as a form of development aid. But if the Brady approach is to become a full-fledged plan, cooperation by both creditors and debtors is needed. How such cooperation can be promoted and effectively achieved, as well as the formidable barriers to cooperation, will be the focus of this study.

NOTES

1. See George Macesich, *World Banking and Finance: Cooperation versus Conflict* (New York: Praeger, 1984), pp. 139ff.

2. World Bank, *Development Report* (Washington: World Bank, 1983). See also *The Economist* (July 30, 1983), p. 61.

3. See "Creditor Nations Urged to Renew Debtor Reform," *Wall Street Journal* (April 24, 1989), p. B5B.

4. Unlike a domestic firm, a foreign country *may* not become insolvent, although it can become illiquid. The qualification is necessary because regimes and dynasties come and go in countries. Not all pay their debts, as many a foreign bondholder has learned to his sorrow. Capacity to pay and willingness to do so are not necessarily identical.

5. See European Investment Bank, *Cahiers BEI/EIB Papers* (March 1989), no. 8, pp. 18–21.

6. Carl Gewirtz, "Gambit for Third World Debt Burden: Baker's Plan Linked to Exports," *International Herald Tribune* (June 21, 1989), pp. 11 and 15.

2 The Theory and Strategy of Cooperation

THE THEORY

How can the necessary cooperation between debtors and creditors for a mutually satisfactory solution to the debt issue come about? For insights into the issues involved, we turn to the theory of cooperation and a strategy of TIT-FOR-TAT. This study draws on the theory of cooperation with reciprocity and a strategy for its implementation as a useful approach in dealing with the global debt issue.

If the 1980s have demonstrated that, through market-oriented reforms in various countries, the marketplaces can find ways to accomplish changes in the world economy without the benefit of conscious actions by planners and governments, relations between developed and developing countries can be described as an area where independent, egoistic nations face each other in a state of near-anarchy. Can developed and developing countries evolve reliable cooperative strategies? Can cooperation emerge in a world of sovereign states? In short, can cooperation evolve out of noncooperation? Specifically, how can cooperation get started at all? Can cooperation strategies survive better than their rivals? Which cooperative strategies will do best, and how will they come to predominate?

Figure 2.1
Prisoner's Dilemma

A = Developed/Creditor Nations

B = Developing/Debtor Nations

Nations A	Nations B	
C Cooperation	R = 3,3 Mutual cooperation	S = 0,5 Sucker's payoff
D Defection	T = 5.0 Temptation to defect	P = 1,1 Punishment for mutual defection

The Game is defined by $T > R > P > S$ and $R > (S+T)/2$.

Many of the problems facing these nations take the form of an iterated Prisoner's Dilemma.[1] In the Prisoner's Dilemma game, two individuals, or nations, can either cooperate or defect. The payoff to a player is in terms of the effect in relation to the payoff. No matter what the other does, the selfish choice of defection yields a higher payoff than cooperation. But if both defect, both do worse than if both had cooperated.

For illustration, let us assume that A (developed/creditor nations) and B (developing/debtor nations) in Figure 2.1 agree to trade. Both are satisfied as to the amounts they will be getting and receiving. Assume further that for some reason, the exchange is to take place in secret. Both agree to place money in a designated location. Let us also assume that neither A nor B will ever meet again or have furtive dealings.

If both A and B carry out their agreement, both stand to gain. It is also obvious that if neither A nor B carried out the agreement, neither would have what it wanted. It is equally obvious if only one carried out its end of the bargain, say A, B would receive something for nothing, since they will never again meet nor have further dealings. There is thus an incentive for both A and B to leave nothing. As a result, neither A nor B gets what it initially wanted. Does the logic prevent cooperation? That is the Prisoner's Dilemma.

The iterated Prisoner's Dilemma can be made more quantitative and in that form be studied by the methods of game theory and computer simulation. In order to do this, we build a "payoff" matrix presenting hypothetical values for the various alternatives, such as Figure 2.1.

In this matrix mutual cooperation by A and B yields to both parties three points. Mutual defection yields to both zero points. If A cooperates but B does not, B gets five points, because it is better to get something for nothing. The number 3 is called the "reward for cooperation" R. The number 1 is called the "punishment" or P. The number 5 is T for "temptation," and 0 is S, the "sucker's" payoff. The conditions necessary for the matrix to represent a Prisoner's Dilemma are the following:

$$T > R > S \qquad 2.1$$

$$\frac{T+S<R}{2} \qquad 2.2$$

The first condition (2.1) says that it is better to defect no matter what the other side does. The second condition (2.2) in effect guarantees that if A and B get locked into out-of-phase alternatives (e.g., A cooperates but B defects in one period and B cooperates but A defects in the second period), A will not do better. In fact, A will do worse than if A cooperated in each period.

If A and B will never meet again, an unlikely situation in our example, the only appropriate solution indicated by the game is to defect always. This strategy is correct even though both could do better if they cooperated. Thus, in an iterated Prisoner's Dilemma played only once, to defect is always the best strategy.

In an iterated Prisoner's Dilemma game where the same two participants may meet more than once, a much greater set of options is available. A strategy would include a decision rule that determined the probability of cooperation or defection as a function of the history of interaction thus far. However, if there is a known number of interactions between a pair of individuals, to defect always is still evolutionarily stable; that is, individuals using the strategy of defection cannot do better by another strategy. The reason is that the defection on the last interaction would be optimal for both sides. Of course, so would defection on the next to the last interaction and on back to the first.

On the other hand, if the number of interactions is not fixed in advance but is given by some probability, W, that after the first interaction, the same two individuals (nations) will meet again, other strategies become evolutionary stable as well. Indeed, when W is sufficiently great, there is no single best strategy, regardless of the behavior of the others in the population. The matter, however, is not hopeless.

In fact, Axelrod and Hamilton demonstrate that there is a strategy that is stable, robust, and viable. Accordingly, the evolution of cooperation can be conceptualized in three separate questions:

1. *Robustness*. What type of strategy can thrive in a variegated environment composed of others using a wide variety of more or less sophisticated strategies?
2. *Stability*. Under what conditions can such a strategy, once fully established, resist invasion by mutant strategies?
3. *Initial viability*. Even if a strategy is robust and stable, how can it ever get a foothold in an environment that is predominantly noncooperative?[2]

THE STRATEGY

Axelrod and Hamilton submitted various strategies to a computer tournament drawing upon contributors in game theory from economics, mathematics, political science, and sociology. The result of the tournament was that "the highest average score was attained by the simplest of all strategies submitted: TIT-FOR-TAT. This strategy is simply one of cooperating on the first move and then doing what the other player did on the preceding move. Thus, TIT-FOR-TAT is a strategy of cooperation based on reciprocity."[3]

The robustness of TIT-FOR-TAT is reported by the authors as dependent on three features: "It was never the first to defect, it was provocable into retaliation by a defection of the other, and it was forgiving after just one act of retaliation. . . . In the long run, TIT-FOR-TAT displaced all other rules and went to fixation" and so provides "further evidence that TIT-FOR-TAT's cooperation based on reciprocity is a robust strategy that can thrive in a variegated environment."[4]

The authors then demonstrate that once TIT-FOR-TAT has gone to fixation, it can resist invasion by any possible mutant strategy provided that individuals who interact have a sufficiently large probability, W, of meeting again.

Since TIT-FOR-TAT is not the only strategy that can be evolutionarily stable, it raises the problem of how an evolutionary trend to cooperative behavior could ever have started in the first place. Axelrod and Hamilton provide several illustrations when benefits of cooperation can be harvested by groups of closely related individuals.

Clustering can also lead to a TIT-FOR-TAT strategy even when virtually everyone is using an ALL D (defection) strategy. Suppose that a small group of individuals is using TIT-FOR-TAT and that a certain proportion, p, of the interactions of the members of this cluster are with other members of the cluster. Then, the average score attained by members of the cluster using TIT-FOR-TAT strategy is

$$p\,[R/(1 - W)] + (1 - p)\,[S + WP/(1 - W)] \qquad 2.3$$

If the members of the cluster provide a negligible proportion of the interactions for the other individuals, then the score attained by those using ALL D is still $P/(1-W)$. When p and w are large enough, a cluster of TIT-FOR-TAT individuals can become initially viable in an environment composed overwhelmingly of ALL D.

Can the reverse happen? That is, once a strategy of TIT-FOR-TAT becomes established, can it be displaced? According to the authors, the answer is no. This is because the score achieved by the strategy that comes in a cluster is a weighted average of how it does with others of its kind and with the predominant strategy. Each of these components is less than or equal to the score achieved by TIT-FOR-TAT. Thus, the strategy arriving in a cluster cannot intrude on TIT-FOR-TAT. In other words, when W is large enough to make TIT-FOR-TAT an evolutionary stable strategy, it can resist intrusion by any cluster of any other strategy.

In summation, "cooperation based on reciprocity can get started in a predominantly noncooperative world, can thrive in a variegated environment, and can defend itself once fully established. . . . The gear wheels of social evolution have a ratchet."[5]

It is noteworthy for our purposes that TIT-FOR-TAT won the various tournament games not by beating the other player but by eliciting behavior from the other player that allowed both to do well. Indeed, it was so consistent in generating mutually rewarding results that it achieved a higher overall score than any other strategy in the tournament.

So-called non-nice or tricky strategies designed to sound out how much an opponent "minded" being defected against typically backfired, causing severe breakdowns of trust. In other words, attempts to use defection in a game to "flush out" an opponent's weak spots turned out to be very costly. It proved more profitable to have a policy of cooperation as often as possible, together with a willingness to retaliate swiftly in a restrained and forgiving manner.

Furthermore, the best approach is straightforwardness and simplicity. Being so complex as to be incomprehensible is very dangerous indeed. Too complex a strategy can appear to be chaotic. A random strategy can appear to be unresponsive to the other player. An unresponsive strategy provides no incentive for the other player to cooperate.

The significance of these results for the ongoing dialogue between our developing/debtor countries and developed/creditor countries is obvious. It is not surprising that the Byzantine strategies followed by some participants in the dialogue have so little to show in the way of concrete results.

Among the important lessons for our developed/developing nations' dialogue derived from Axelrod's tournament efforts is that previously game theorists did not take their analysis far enough. That is, it is important to minimize echo effects in an environment of mutual power. He argues that a sophisticated analysis calls for going three levels deep. The first is the direct effect of a choice. Since a defection always earns more than cooperation, this is easy. The second involves the indirect effects of the other side punishing or not punishing a defection. The third level comprises the response to the defections of the other side in which one may repeat or even amplify one's own exploitative choice. Thus, a single defection may be successful when considered for its direct effects and perhaps even in its secondary effects. The tertiary effects, however, may be the real costs when one's own single defection turns into unending mutual recriminations. In effect, many of the rules actually wind up punishing themselves. The other player simply serves as a mechanism to delay the self-punishment by a few moves.

In essence, there is much to be learned about coping in an environment of mutual power. Indeed, Axelrod reports that many expert strategists from economics, political science, mathematics, sociology, and psychology made the systematic error of being too competitive for their own good, not forgiving enough and too pessimistic about the responsiveness of the other side.

In a non-zero-sum world, a nation does not have to do better than another player nation to do well for itself. The more player nations are interacting, the better. As long as A does well, it is all right if the others do as well or a little better. It is pointless for A to be envious of the success of another country, because in an iterated Prisoner's Dilemma of long duration, the success of the other is virtually a prerequisite of A's doing well for itself.

Clearly this principle holds for our debtor and creditor countries. A country that borrows from another can expect that the loan will be mutually beneficial. There is no point in the borrower's being envious of the creditor's terms and interest. Any attempt to reduce it through an uncooperative practice, such as not making interest and principal payments on time or as agreed, will only encourage the creditor to take retaliatory action. Retaliatory action could take many forms, often without being explicitly labeled as punishment—poorer credit ratings, less prompt deliveries of needed materials, fewer discounts, and, in general, less favorable market conditions for the debtor country's goods and services. In short, the retaliation could make the envy quite expensive. Instead of worrying about the relative profits of the creditor, the debtor should worry about whether another borrowing strategy would be better. For instance, it can lift domestic restrictions on interest paid on savings and bank deposits, thereby mobilizing greater domestic savings, which would reduce external borrowing requirements.

The significance of the environment for the endogenous evolution of institutions à la Hayek is evident in the results reported by Axelrod and others in the "ecological tournament."[6] The tournament consists not only of single subjunctive replay but also of our entire cascade of hypothetical replays, each one's environment determined by the preceding replay. In particular, if you take a program's score in a tournament as a measure of its "fitness," and if you interpret "fitness" to mean "number of progeny in the next generation," and, finally, if you let "next generations" mean "next tournament," then what you get is that each tournament's results determine the environment of the next tournament. This type of iterated tournament is called ecological because it stimulates ecological adaptation, the shifting of a fixed set of species' populations according to their mutually defined and dynamically developing environment, as contrasted with the mutation-oriented aspects of evolution, where new species can come into existence.

Carrying the ecological tournament generation after generation results in gradual change in the environment. At the start, poor and good programs are equally represented. As the tournament goes on, the poorer programs drop out while the good ones remain. The rank order of the good ones will now change since the field of competitors has changed.

In short, success breeds success only if the successful programs are permitted to interact. If, in contrast, the success of some programs is due mostly to their ability to exploit less successful programs, then as these exploitation-prone programs are gradually squeezed out, the exploiter's base of support is eroded, and the exploiter too will fall out. As Axelrod points out, playing with rules that do not score well is eventually self-defeating. Not being nice may look promising at the start, but in the long run its effect is to destroy the very environment upon which its success depends.

Consider now the ongoing dialogue between developed and developing countries against our theory of cooperation outlined above. Cooperation based on reciprocity can gain a foothold through at least two different mechanisms. One is "kinship," or closely related individuals or institutions. Banks and the debtor/creditor relationship of about $1.3 trillion between developing and developed nations constitute such a relationship.

A second mechanism to overcome a strategy of total defection (ALL D) is for the mutant strategy, cooperation, to arrive in such a cluster so as to provide a nontrivial proportion of the interaction each has. In addition to the $1.3 trillion debt/credit relationship between developing and developed nations, the extensive trade relations that now make for increasing world interdependence provide such a cluster.

As reported by Axelrod and Hamilton, a computer tournament approach will demonstrate that a strategy of TIT-FOR-TAT will fare better than alternative strategies. It is robust. It does well in a variety of circumstances. It is stable, especially against a wide variety of mutant strategies. Cooperation can indeed prosper. It can emerge in a world of egoists without central control by starting with a cluster of individuals/nations who rely on reciprocity.

In short, advice given to players of the Prisoner's Dilemma might also serve world bankers, as well as national leaders and others in developed and developing nations, in dealing with one another: Don't be envious, don't be the first to defect, reciprocate both defection and cooperation, and don't be too clever.

To be sure, our application and extension of cooperation theory to the complex arena of international finance and activities of debtor and creditor countries must recognize existing realities in these countries. In particular, we must take into account three critical issues: (1) the domestic constraints within which domestic governments of participant countries operate; (2) the role of economic nationalism; and (3) the interests and motivations of the bureaucratic and political elite in general. This study focuses on these issues.

NOTES

1. Robert Axelrod and Douglas Dion, "The Further Evolution of Cooperation," *Science* (December 9, 1988), pp. 1385–1389; Robert Axelrod and William D. Hamilton, "The Evolution of Cooperation," *Science* (March 27, 1981), pp. 1390–1396; Douglas R. Hofstadter, "Metamagical Themas," *Scientific American* (May 1983), pp. 16–26; Anton Rapoport and A. M. Chammah, *Prisoner's Dilemma* (Ann Arbor: University of Michigan Press, 1965); D. Luce and H. Raiffa, *Games and Decisions* (New York: Wiley, 1957), pp. 94–102; M. Cohen, T. Nagel, and T. Scanlon, eds., *War and Moral Responsibility* (Princeton: Princeton University Press, 1974); B. Belassa and R. Nelson, eds., *Economic Progress, Private Values, and Public Policy: Essays in Honor of William Felver* (Amsterdam: North-Holland, 1977); M. Taylor, *Anarchy and Cooperation* (New York: Wiley, 1976); Robert Axelrod, *Evolution of Cooperation* (New York: Basic Books, 1984); Andrew Schotter, *The Economic Theory of Social Institutions* (Cambridge: Cambridge University Press, 1981); Andrew Schotter and Gerhard Schwodiauer, "Economics and the Theory of Games: A Survey," *Journal of Economic Literature* (June 1980), pp. 479–527; George Macesich, *World Banking and Finance: Cooperation versus Conflict* (New York: Praeger, 1984); George Macesich, *Monetary Reform and Cooperation Theory* (New York: Praeger, 1989).

2. Axelrod and Hamilton, "Evolution of Cooperation," p. 1393. The strategy of TIT-FOR-TAT was submitted to the tournament by Professor Anatol

Rapoport, a psychologist and philosopher at the University of Toronto.

3. Axelrod and Hamilton, "Evolution of Cooperation," p. 1393.

4. Axelrod and Hamilton, "Evolution of Cooperation," p. 1393.

5. Axelrod and Hamilton, "Evolution of Cooperation," p. 1394.

6. The discussion in the following two paragraphs draws on Hofstadter, "Metamagical Themas," pp. 24–25.

3 Domestic Constraints in Debtor Countries

In applying our cooperation theory, it is useful to consider the economic and sociocultural constraints that many debtor countries—located mostly in the Third World—face in dealing with their debt. The tasks before these countries is truly formidable. What many of them lack is virtually everything necessary for a high standard of economic productivity. What is worse, various estimates suggest that there has been a net transfer of resources from the poor south, where many of the debtor countries are located, to the prosperous northern country creditors of over $25 billion a year in the later years of the 1980s.

Many of these debtor countries risk lurching further into darkness. Many of them have seen their already low standards of living decline during the 1980s, and, for the poorest among them, there is no realistic prospect of regaining the social and economic advances they had made earlier. In all except a few countries, malnutrition is increasing as health and education provision declines. Investment is not keeping up with the demand for new jobs, and in some cases, it is declining. This chapter discusses important internal economic and sociocultural constraints on economic development and nation building in many of the debtor countries.

ECONOMIC CONSTRAINTS

In considering the economic constraints which many debtor countries face, it is useful to compare and contrast the circumstances in these countries today with that of the developed creditor countries at the time of their takeoff with sustained economic growth. I have discussed elsewhere the unfortunate coincidence of troubles that brought the collapse of the interwar monetary and financial organizations.[1] Let us turn now to the fortunate coincidence of circumstances that thrust these Western creditor market-oriented countries into sustained economic growth. These fortunate circumstances are by and large economic, political, sociological, and technological.

Consider first the economic circumstances that can be summarized as capital accumulation, population growth, natural resources, and technological advance. Theories of economic development, in essence, provide us with scenarios about the interrelationships of these factors. They attempt to explain economic growth in terms of some causal factors. They differ from models of economic growth that take economic growth as given and simply work out the implications of particular kinds of behavior that are postulated but typically not explained.

In terms of capital accumulation, net savings and investment in today's developed countries averaged 10 to 20 percent of national income during their periods of rapid development. For many Third World debtor countries, net savings and investments today are in the range of 5 to 10 percent of national income—thanks to low levels of national incomes, not enough to provide a critical level of savings and investments necessary to surmount the problem of economic development in these countries.

On the issue of population growth, the developed countries were thrust into development long before their population explosion. The Third World debtor countries, on the other hand, have already experienced, and indeed are experiencing, population explosion before they are firmly launched into development.

In fact, Simon Kuznets, in his book on economic growth structure, underscores six significant differences between the now developing countries and developed countries when they began their development:[2] (1) The present level of per capita product in the underdeveloped countries is much lower than it was in the now developed countries with the possible single exception of Japan; (2) the supply of land per capita is much smaller in the developing countries currently than it was in the present advanced countries when they began their development; (3) agricultural productivity in developing countries today is probably lower than it was in the advanced countries in the past; (4) the inequality in the distribution of income is wider today than in the past, but not in a way that favors accumulation of productive capital; (5) the social and political structure of the low-income countries currently is a much greater barrier than it was in the past; (6) most of the present-day underdeveloped countries are attempting development after a long period of colonial status, whereas many currently developed countries launched development after many years of political independence.[3]

Natural resources and technological advance are other elements with which some Third World debtor countries are in difficulty. Both elements require entrepreneurship if they are to be properly developed and effectively introduced into the economy. Unfortunately, the entrepreneurial spirit appears limited—at least by comparison with the upsurge of enterprise that characterized contemporary developed countries during the eighteenth and nineteenth centuries. Attempts by government to replace private enterprise as innovator and entrepreneur have not been met with ringing success. The human capital so necessary for the implementation and generation of technological progress and economic development is, simply, in very short supply in the Third World.

Although it may be possible to accelerate technological advance so as to aid development in the Third World, it is not likely that the fortunate coincidence of circumstances that so favored the developed countries of today will be repeated. Population that grew from levels below optimal in the developed countries and so stimulated development has thus far had a retarding effect on development in the Third World. Technological advance that is by and large concentrated in the developed countries is not in tune with the needs and requirements of the Third World.

Political and economic factors combined in the eighteenth and nineteenth centuries to assist the contemporary developed countries. Consider, for instance, the significant role that Great Britain played in the nineteenth century in assisting these countries; it is all too often brushed aside in the Third World's condemnation of imperialism and colonialism. It would be helpful to compare the policies of the United States and the Soviet Union in the postwar period with that of Great Britain, particularly after the Napoleonic Wars and the Congress of Vienna in 1815.[4]

In foreign investment it has been estimated that, in the early 1950s, if the United States, for instance, had lent abroad on a scale equivalent in per capita real income to that of Great Britain during the nineteenth century, it would have had a $600-billion foreign investment in 1952 that would have earned it $30 billion a year.[5] At the peak of its empire in the last third of the nineteenth century, Great Britain invested about 40 percent of its savings abroad. Comparable U.S. capital outflow would be about $30 billion a year, as contrasted with an actual net private outflow of some $1 billion to $3 billion. Prior to World War I, Great Britain obtained about one-tenth of its income from returns on overseas investment. British investment during the pre–World War I period was roughly twice the French and more than twice the German investment. More than half of the British foreign investment was outside the Empire, especially in the United States and Latin America.[6] At the same time, Great Britain actively followed a policy of free trade, in contrast to the relatively high tariff policy of the United States. One can argue that Great Britain followed a policy of free trade for reasons of good state policy. It had a virtual monopoly on manufactured products while enjoying nearly a monopsony in the purchase of raw materials and food from abroad. Such a "monopoly-monopsony" position is not, however, enjoyed by the United States, a fact that partly explains the U.S. tariff policy. Great Britain's policy of free trade may have served to accelerate development abroad, whereas U.S. protectionist policy may serve to retard such development.

Although British private investment abroad was dominant, it was consistent with British government policy. Thus one can argue that the French Revolution provided the British government with an incentive to treat the average British citizen to more consideration than in the past lest Britons, too, revolt.[7] One way, of course, was to obtain cheap food from abroad. Frontier developments using British capital made cheaper food possible. In effect, assisting economic development abroad was not only good economics but good politics as well.

So, too, with the motivation behind a significant fraction of U.S. government-to-government aid in the immediate postwar period. Various commentators have examined these motivations which seemed to range from underlying humanitarian impulses on the part of the wealthy U.S. society at one extreme, to the direct lure of increased export markets on the other. However, the consensus places greatest emphasis on the importance of American political and security interests in the Cold War confrontation with the Soviet Union. This is consistent with the concentration of 80 percent of total U.S. aid on countries around the periphery of the Soviet Union and its friends. Moreover, aid programs have invariably been presented to the U.S. Congress as measures designed to prevent one or another country from falling to Soviet infiltration or takeover. There has also been a noticeable fluctuation in the size of aid packages according to the intensity of U.S.–Soviet rivalry. Aid-giving is thus viewed basically as a product of enlightened self-interest.

There is, moreover, the fact stressed by some observers that Great Britain when dealing abroad did so largely with its own citizens, so that physical and political control followed overseas investment.[8] In any case, the other major world powers, such as France, Germany, the Netherlands, and Austria-Hungary, had an interest in preserving peace and tranquility in the then-developing regions. In contrast, today political control of investment across national frontiers is very difficult to exercise. Competition between the United States and the Soviet Union for friends and influence in the Third World assures something less than tranquility in the developing countries, even though the stated goal is their growth and stability.

SOCIOCULTURAL CONSTRAINTS

As we have discussed, the developing countries of yesteryear were much more similar in their sociocultural makeup to the developed countries. They shared attitudes, values, and language, and responded to the same incentives as the developed countries, such as Great Britain. Today the situation is very different—the one shared characteristic is diversity.

The sociocultural environment of a country includes language, religion, values, attitudes, and education, among other important elements. As for culture, it is a durable concept. It is incorporated into the disciplines of anthropology, sociology, political science, history, geography, and economics.[9]

Consider the issue of language and whether a country is homogenous or heterogeneous linguistically. Although linguistic heterogeneity does not necessarily result in underdevelopment—witness, for example, developed Switzerland and Belgium—more than sixty of the current developing countries do not share a common language.[10] The fact is that a multiplicity of languages in a country tends to hinder economic integration and market size, thereby reducing the division of labor and the possibilities for economies of scale. This also may result in fragmentation of political life and may lead to internal instability. Indeed, scholars have often commented on the fragile nature of heterogeneous societies, particularly when such societies are placed under pressures of rapid development.[11]

India is an example of linguistic heterogeneity and its associated problems.[12] No less than fifteen languages are listed, along with several hundred other languages of varying degrees of importance. Fortunately, many of these language groups are concentrated in compact regions and organized into constituent states of a federation.

Obviously aware of the difficulties presented by linguistic plurality, many developing countries have opted for the promotion of a uniform strategy by using a single official language for administration, usually the language inherited from the colonial power. This option, too, has problems, since the former colonial powers typically promoted uniformity by using their own language as the official language.

Indeed, the newer states in Africa and Asia are confronted with the practical issue of what to do about the foreign official language inherited from the colonial power. On the one hand, there are strong reasons against maintaining the colonial language. One issue is that language is a symbol of national identity and independence. Another issue is that the colonial language is often associated with antidemocratic elements of the past. More important is the view that the colonial language may hinder communication between authorities and the rest of the population and so create a barrier for carrying out various development programs. Another is that education is best carried out in the mother tongue. Finally, a foreign language may be a barrier to development of a nation's cultural life. Still other reasons could be added for discouraging continuation of the foreign colonial language.

Nonetheless, there are also powerful reasons for maintaining the colonial language. One, of course, is simple inertia, since the language has typically been around for a good many years, especially with the elite, bureaucracy, higher education, and other important elements in the life of a nation. In addition, there is the practical issue of finding a suitable substitute language, since choosing one of perhaps several tongues in a country presents other problems. Moreover, the former colonial language is typically a modern language capable of meeting the requirements of modern commerce, industry, technology, and education in general, thereby providing the country with access to the currents of development.

The pressure of events usually forces the developing countries to opt for one of the world's major languages, typically English. There are, however, strong counterpressures in the form of cultural independence and national identity. The resolution of these problems is not easy—certainly not for a fledgling nation in the first euphoria of independence.

The adoption of English, if not as the country's primary language then certainly as its second language, has many advantages for a nation aspiring to participate in the world economy. It is a legacy not only of the British Empire but also of U.S. economic, technological, and military power, especially in the post–World War II era. Indeed, in Europe, English is more widely spoken as a second language than is any other language, including French.[13]

As a matter of fact, evidence of the important role of English in the Third World was provided at the Bandung Conference in 1955: English was the official language of the conference. The Soviet Union and China, among others, beam their broadcasts to the Third World in English. English, then, is an important factor in aiding development in the Third World, just as it has been for more than a hundred years in the British Dominions and the United States.

The importance of religion in the cultural environment and as a determinant in many of the external manifestations of culture should not be minimized. Much behavior can stem from the religion of the country's culture—for example, the role of women, educational systems, social relations, and political organization. The Judeo-Christian tradition and ideas contained in the Reformation and the Calvinist and Puritan ethic were shared by the developing Western countries of two hundred years ago. Today the situation is very different.

Consider the effects that five of the major religions have on economic behavior and the economy of the Third World: animism, Hinduism, Buddhism, Islam, and Christianity. A quick survey of per capita income will suggest that the world's Protestant nations have the highest, followed by the Catholic countries. The Muslim nations are in the next category, with the Buddhist and Hindu countries in the lowest group.[14] The animistic or nonliterate religious societies, largely in Africa, are more mixed, in that a literate religion, such as Christianity or Islam, coexists with them.

The role of religion in economic development has been treated by many scholars, and there is little point in reporting their results except to emphasize that religion is important even in so-called sectarian societies. It affects a society's values, attitudes, achievement, and motivation in general. Its divisive nature is also only too visible in countries torn apart through religious heterogeneity, as in Northern Ireland between Protestants and Roman Catholics and in the Indian subcontinent between Muslims and Hindus. No continent is spared the tragedy of religious clashes—witness Africa with Muslim pressures on Christians and the Near East with the Arab and Jewish tragedy.

Let us then examine briefly the five major religions noted above insofar as they impinge on economic development. Consider, first, animism, which is thought by many to be mankind's oldest religion. Sometimes seen as primitive religion or nonliterate religion, it is often described as the view of nature as animated by indwelling spirits. This appears to have preceded the view of religion as controlled by external deities; in effect, animism precedes deism.[15] More than thirty developing countries in the Third World can cite animism as a major religious factor. Most of these countries are located in Africa, south of the Sahara. Five are in Latin America, where their animism is mixed with Roman Catholicism. The only Asian country listed is Laos, where Buddhism is dominant.

The important point is that animistic societies tend to be strongly conservative and tradition oriented. As a result, new products and techniques are not easily adopted. Efforts to introduce new methods into agriculture, for instance, will quite likely meet strong resistance. Moreover, the belief in magic in these societies limits the appeal of science and indeed the scientific method, and a vast and expensive reeducation program is required if development is to take place with modern techniques. It should be no surprise that these societies are also the least developed in the Third World.

Hinduism is difficult to describe as a religion. It is often described as a way of life. As a result, it is even more difficult to change since one is not confronted with a religious dogma but instead with a way of life developed over a period of more than four thousand years on the Indian subcontinent.[16] To understand India, where more than 80 percent of the total population of over 500 million are Hindus, one must attempt to understand Hinduism.

Although the practice of Hinduism varies widely from class to class and from region to region, several issues do stand out. For instance, unlike Christianity and Islam, Hinduism is not a creedal religion. This means that practices tend to be important. Intuition, experience, and inward realization are more important than intellect, dogma, and outer experience in Hinduism. Its strength and durability is the ability to assimilate and adapt so as to become "all things to all men."

The impact of Hinduism on the economy cannot be very positive. For instance, the caste system, which was originally a color bar, is tied up with labor mobility, for instance, between occupations. But the caste and subcaste system involves more than simply occupation or indeed social class as these terms are normally understood. The differentiation is much stronger. Perhaps a better descriptive word is "species." Legislation, such as in the Indian constitution, outlawing discrimination based on caste does not readily change social behavior whose roots are in four thousand years of history.

The extended family, or "Baradari," is a source of stability and strength in society. Many Indian enterprises, for instance, are family endeavors based on family relationships rather than on modern Western organizational concepts. Nepotism in India has a positive value. Consumption, too, is a joint-family issue, unlike the case in the Western single family or household unit.[17] However, it would be inaccurate to argue that modernization under Hinduism is impossible. Witness, for example, India's two centuries of progress and development—under British influence, to be sure.

Progress, nevertheless, has created a Hindu elite capable of sustaining such progress. D. K. Rangnekar aptly summarized the Indian problem in the following:

> The young Indian must come round to a rational and objective view of material advancement. He must be able and willing to tear himself away from family ties; flout customs and traditions; put economic welfare before cow worship; think in terms of farm and factory output rather than in terms of gold and silver ornaments; spend on tools and training rather than on temples and ceremonials; work with the low caste rather than starve with the high caste; think of the future rather than of the past; concentrate on material gains rather than dwell on Kismet (destiny). These are extremely difficult changes to envisage in the Hindu social structure and ideas. But they seem unavoidable.[18]

In contrast to the complexities of Hinduism, Buddhism is relatively simple and straightforward in teaching and practice. This does not mean that diversity does not exist in Buddhism, for it most certainly does, as in all major religions. Two divisions of Buddhism (Theravada Buddhists in South and East Asia and Mahayana Buddhists in North Asia) number about 200 million people. Like Hinduism, Buddhism is more than a religion in the Western sense. It is a lifestyle, an all-encompassing element of spiritual, cultural, and political identity. Buddhism emphasizes wantlessness and contemplation rather than consumption and work.[19] Although it may not be world denying, it is questionable how world affirming Buddhism is in terms of economic development. For instance, the Buddhist countries of Southeast Asia are among the lesser developed members of the Third World.

In the Northern Asian countries of China, Japan, Korea, Mongolia, Tibet, and Nepal, where Mahayana Buddhism exists, it does so alongside Taoism and Confucianism in China and Shintoism in Japan. As a result, Buddhism is diluted and modified, and its impact on the economies of these countries is difficult to ascertain.

No single event in world history during the millennium between the fall of Rome and the European voyages of discovery was more significant than the rise of Islam. Thanks to OPEC and oil, Islam is again a force to be reckoned with and so has drawn particular world attention. Islam is the religion of more than 500 million people, with the majority living in the Third World and primarily in Asia, the Middle East, and Africa. In Europe and other regions, Islam is a minority religion. Conquest and the force of arms account for its spread, although Islam's preferred absence of racial discrimination very likely had appeal, especially in India, where most of the converts were of lower caste. Brotherhood and equality as preached by Islam proved attractive in other places as well.

As strong as Islam's appeal is in the Third World countries, it, too, is more than a religion; it also involves legislation that organizes all human relationships. The Shariah, or law of Islam, includes every detail of human life, not only state organizations but also personal and social relations and actions. Unlike other countries, Muslim nations are established as religious states wherein each citizen accepts full responsibility for the performance of his religious duties and the observance of the Shariah. No distinction in Muslim countries exists between the secular and religious. Indeed, the Muslim name for citizen is *mukallaf*, which means one who accepts responsibility for carrying out duties laid out by the Shariah.

No formal clergy exists in Islam, only scholars who are experts in the sacred book of Koran and traditions, Hadith, that have grown up alongside it. These influential scholars, or *ulama* or *ulema*, as they are called, play a very important role as both teachers and preachers. One result of such influence is that *ulema* may serve to provide or discourage change and so encourage or retard economic development.

The foundations of Islam rest on five pillars:

1. *The profession of faith*: "There is no God but Allah, and Mohammed is His Prophet."
2. *Prayer*: Practiced five times a day, according to a set ritual.
3. *Fasting*: Done during daylight hours in the month of Ramadan.
4. *Almsgiving*: One traditionally donates a portion of one's income.
5. *The hajj*: A pilgrimage to Mecca is made once during one's lifetime.

To judge from available evidence, Muslim countries tend to be at the lower end of economic development. Those with oil resources, of course, are experiencing a significant period of growth in the GNP as well as a general revival. However, other indicators of development tend to confirm the general backwardness of these countries. For instance, the literacy rate is significantly below 50 percent. So, too, is newspaper circulation. Population density is low and so is the productivity of agriculture. The general picture, in effect, is one of rural backwardness, with a high percentage of the population engaged in primitive agriculture. This is a sad commentary indeed, for from the ninth to the fourteenth centuries, Muslim teachers and researchers kept alive and extended the range of Greek science and strengthened the bases of modern science.

Insallah, or "God willing," is the orthodox belief that everything good or evil proceeds directly from the divine will, being irrevocably recorded on the Preserved Tablet. This fatalism, along with the pervasive impact of Islam, is considered by many observers to be the major cause of the lack of economic progress in Muslim countries. For instance, Insallah conflicts with the idea of insurance, which can be viewed as working against Allah's will. As a result, world banks may find themselves financing uninsured projects, including inventories. So, too, is the prohibition against charging interest for loans, though this is typically circumvented by charging commission instead. However, if a bank must

go to court to collect, it may well be faced with a Muslim court decision awarding only the loan principal.

In essence, Islamic countries are at a crossroads today. They must choose whether to deny the essentials of Islam and opt for a secular state or go through the difficult struggle of trying to produce an Islamic order or an Islamic state. The struggle is reminiscent of the conflicts between the medieval Roman church and the emerging European nation-states. Islam is six hundred years younger than Christianity. These choices will not be made easier by a leadership split among professional politicians who are essentially secular, Westernized, and non-Islamic and who simply jump on the Islamic bandwagon to achieve their political goals.

The *ulema* constitute the second group; they are the professional men of religion—conservative and traditionalist, having committed themselves to the preservation of Islam so that it is, in fact, a living tradition. They are to be found in the political, cultural, and educational life of all Muslim countries. Moreover, they are organized and their efforts are productive. Examples are such organizations as the Nahdatuh Ulema in Indonesia; in Pakistan, the Jamaat i Ulema i Islam and the Jamaat i Ulema i Pakistan; in Cairo, sheiks of Al Azlar; in Morocco, the Rahitat Ulema al Maghreb; and finally the entire body of sheiks in countries, such as Saudi Arabia, that claim to be Islamic states.

Another group, though presumably Westernized, are really not "Westernizers" so much as they are modernizers. They claim to be Islamic believers but reject the more fundamentalist interpretation. They appear to be the most serious and most important factor in the upsurge of Islam in the post–World War II period. They have taken it upon themselves to rethink Islam in modern terms.

These people and organizations vary widely in their approach and objectives. Some want an Islamic society within an Islamic state based on the Koran and Sunnah; others want an Islamic society within an Islamic order, derived from the Koran and the Sunnah; some accept violence and others do not. The element that seems to unite all these elements is the desire to make Islam relevant to the contemporary world.

However, education is the most critical element in any successful Islamic thrust into the post–World War II period. Regarding their Muslim subjects, it is also the issue on which the former colonial powers appear to have agreed—namely, to give their colonial subjects as little education as possible, and the wrong kind, at that. The introduction of wholly Westernized and wholly European education systems buttressed

by European languages was aimed at providing a minimal colonial administration. The minorities were largely ignored so that those aspiring to such an education went abroad. They returned as aliens in their own societies.

The most significant change in these societies in the postwar period is that their educational systems at all levels have once again reinstituted the teaching of Islam in the curricula. It is this Islamization of the young since the postwar period, coupled with the shedding of colonial authority, that has again brought Islam into confrontation with the rest of the world.

Indeed, confrontation between Islam and the rest of the world has been an on-again, off-again issue for almost fifteen hundred years. We need but recall the Crusades of the eleventh and twelfth centuries and the Moors in Spain; the fall of the Serbian Empire at the Battles of Marica in 1371 and Kosovo in 1389, which opened Europe to Ottoman incursions; the fall of Constantinople in 1453 to the Muslims which marked the end of the Byzantine Empire; the establishment by Charles V in 1521 of a military frontier running through present-day Yugoslavia and lasting until 1871 as a defense and containment of Islam; the Ottoman Empire, which included a significant portion of Europe and whose rise encouraged the great European voyages of exploration in search of alternative trade routes to the East, much like today's search for alternative sources of energy; the Balkan Wars of the nineteenth and early twentieth centuries, as well as World War I, which owe their genesis in some part to Islamic incursions into Europe; the Greek and Turkish conflicts; and the Russian experience with Islam over the centuries, which also colors today's response to its resurgence in the Islamic countries of Asia, the Middle East, and Africa.

The Third World movement since World War II has in good measure been propelled by Islam located in the Afro-Asian countries. In fact, without its Afro-Asian contingent and especially its oil-rich OPEC members, the nonaligned movement as a group of nations would have a difficult time remaining together as the Economic Group of 77. Without the Group of 77, the North-South dialogue and demands for a new international economic order (NIEO) would very likely fall on deaf ears.

The Soviet Union, for its part, may have more than 40 million Muslims in Soviet Central Asia and the Caucasus. Although skepticism exists, Soviet incursions into Afghanistan may be explained by a desire to put down the chaos and the spread of Islamic fundamentalism and disintegration in a geopolitical and strategic arena as a historic buffer region. In effect, the spread of volatile, chaotic, unpredictable Islamic anticommunism across Iran, Pakistan, and Afghanistan could very well open up the whole region and thrust U.S. and Chinese power to the frontiers of the Soviet Union. At the same time, a Soviet thrust to the south would place it astride the region, eliminating security dangers and achieving a time-honored desire toward commanding a position in the Indian Ocean and the oil-producing area of the Persian Gulf.

Although the Muslim population's challenge to the Kremlin may not be serious thus far, one can speculate about the future, especially in view of Soviet efforts to involve Muslims more actively in decision making. An educated Muslim elite, together with pressure from a high Soviet Muslim birthrate—which, if it continues, will make Muslims about a quarter of the Soviet population by the end of the century—spells a very potent force, all the more so if coupled with Islamic nationalism. How to counter Islamic nationalism in the Soviet Union may be one of the most serious problems confronting Kremlin leadership to date.

Yugoslavia seems to have done much better in arranging for its Muslim population of 3 million—the result of the high tide of Islamic expansion into Europe. The fact that Yugoslavia has done so places it in good standing in the leadership of the Third World. There are about 1.7 million Bosnian Muslims in Yugoslavia, with the majority living in the republic of Bosnia-Herzegovina. They are descended from Slavs who embraced Islam after the Turkish conquest of Bosnia in 1463. Another 1.3 million are non-Slavic Muslims. In 1968, Muslims were given full nationality status, on a par with the Serbs, Croats, Macedonians, Slovenes, and Yugoslavia's other nationalities. Many mosques have been built in Bosnia-Herzegovina, partly with financing from abroad. Young Muslims are permitted to study abroad in Cairo and other Islamic capitals. Bosnian Muslims do not consider themselves anti-Western but rather as an enlightened and progressive outpost of Islam. Nevertheless, Bosnian Muslim publications have applauded the upsurge of Islam in recent years.

Christianity, whether Orthodox, Roman Catholic, or Protestant, was shared by the developed and developing countries of yesteryear. Such scholars as Max Weber in *The Protestant Ethic and the Spirit of Capitalism*, R. H. Tawney in *Religion and the Rise of Capitalism*, and D. McClelland in *The Achieving Society* have discussed the impact of Christianity on economic development. The point is that religion is important because the influence of religious tradition is so enduring. Through its effects on values, attitudes, and incentives, religion influences the economy.

That values and attitudes toward wealth and material gain are crucial for a country's economy to develop is an idea not universally shared over the world. Indeed, Gunnar Myrdal observes:

> The modernization ideals are all in a sense alien to the region [Asia] since they stem from foreign influences. But they have cause to be indigenous in the sense that they have been adopted and shaped by the intellectual elite, who, in turn, have endeavored to diffuse them throughout the population. The other valuations held by the mass of people and in large part also by the intellectual elite, are mainly "traditional": they use part of an inherited culture long identified with a stagnating society. Related to this is another distinction. While the modernization ideals, both individually and as a system of valuations, are dynamic and interventionist, requiring changes through public policy, all traditional valuations including those on the most intellectualized level are static. Even when they are of such a nature as to lend support to the modernization ideals, they themselves are not the driving force. The static character of the traditional valuations is obvious when they appear as inhibitions and obstacles.[20]

One can reasonably ask whether planners and the intellectual elite have a right to impose their values and attitudes on a developing country as a whole. It is not at all clear that in some Third World countries a consensus on modernization exists. There may well be a preference for stability, tradition, and conservatism purchased at the expense of modernization, economic development, and economic nationalism.

Islam, for instance, contains elements that strongly oppose change. Muhammad is supposed to have said that "all innovation is the work of the devil." Unless the *ulema* who interpret the Koran are favorable to change and development, they may resort to fanatical opposition up to and including assassination of would-be reformers. This has happened in the Muslim Brotherhood in Iran and Egypt.[21] It continues to be a problem in Islamic countries; witness Iran in the 1970s and the overthrow of the shah, who apparently attempted to modernize the country without the blessing and support of Iran's *ulema*.

All of these personal and social risks are in addition to those normally associated with innovation and change. Little wonder that an entrepreneurial spirit is in short supply in these lands. Such attitudes stand in striking contrast to those of the Europeans who undertook the colonization and development burdens of the New World. The fatalism so widespread in many Third World countries simply serves to reinforce attitudes against science, technology, and the scientific method of discovery and problem solving.

This does not mean, of course, that change and development in the Third World is impossible. Economic development need not follow the path of developed countries. Other paths are possible. It does mean that a consensus in those countries regarding development must be reached. It also means that if an evolutionary rather than revolutionary path is chosen, it is necessary to carefully identify those forces serving as impediments to change. Too often change and innovation are attempted before the groundwork is complete, with predictably disastrous results, for example, in Iran. Technical change is likely to be accepted more quickly than, for instance, social or political change, although here, too, we should keep in mind Nehru's observation that "you can't get hold of a modern tool and have an ancient mind. It won't work."

A successful model of change incorporated into a traditional society to meet the needs of a modern industrial country is Japan and the Meiji period, which began in the late 1860s. The traditional values of Japanese society, such as the family system and the emperor system, served both as the motivation for modernization and as justification for sacrifices necessary for social change. These traditional values cushioned the shock of change. Everything undertaken was justified as necessary and in loyal service to the emperor and to one's family. The large industrial organization, or *zaibatsu*, that subsequently developed in Japan rested in good measure on these shared traditional values anchored firmly in the past, which served the country well in its transformation and development into a modern industrial country.

Another element with which the developing countries of yesteryear were not concerned is unionism and unions. In the Third World developing countries, unions are concerned not simply with higher material standards of living but also with political and social issues. In many of these countries, the unions are, for good or bad, politicized. Some, indeed, have served as rallying organizations in the struggle for independence. Reluctance to tolerate other sources of power has caused the unions in some developing countries to become little more than an arm of the government. At times, too, unions in the Third World tend to push for welfare and social programs that some developing countries can ill afford materially.

Education and technology are considered by many economists as prime movers in the course of economic development. They are factors in raising productivity and a more efficient and effective use of available resources. Along with traditional factor inputs of land, labor, and capital, we include education and technology; they are obviously interrelated, especially with such factors as capital. It is also obvious that land, along with the natural resources that it represents, contributes little to economic growth without the application of appropriate technology. In turn, this depends on the education of labor so as to increase its capacity to understand and apply technology, which, in turn, is made possible by the availability of capital. This is, in effect, the well-known interrelationship between labor, land, capital, education, and technology that plays a vital role in promoting a country's economic growth and development.

The application of modern technology and education in an economy has consequences that are seldom fully appreciated by countries in a hurry to develop. For instance, technological change by introducing new methods of production typically requires changes in factor inputs by various industries. As a result, burdens of adjustment may fall unevenly on various factors and sectors of the economy. The country may well find itself undergoing the painful process of structural adjustment, which may have serious political consequences. For instance, not all sectors and segments of the economy and the society may be prepared to accept the necessary adjustment. There is, after all, the natural human instinct to protect oneself and more especially one's way of life. Intuitively and quite correctly, people feel that a change in economic circumstances may portend a change in society. Indeed, it is when society is stepping from one economic structure to another that a crisis is most likely to occur.

It is well known that a great variety of cultural forms are found under any given set of technological and educational conditions. It is also well known that technology and education can, and usually do, interact and serve as powerful influences on a society's culture by providing it with new possibilities and capabilities. Such interaction will very likely have a ripple effect, requiring further cultural changes.

Education and technology serve a country's standing in international trade by influencing its comparative trade and production advantages. In developed countries, technological advances, especially in new synthetic fibers, for example, have had the effect of slowing down the demand for some primary products of Third World countries. Thus it is that a country's comparative advantage and trade position may be critically dependent on technological and educational conditions.

The Third World's technological and educational condition has been variously deplored in discussions of "technological dependence," "technological gap," and "brain drain." Countries fear technological dependence will deprive them of economic development and military and political influence. Such dependence, they worry, will only serve to stunt the development of their domestic managerial and technological capabilities. Usually multinational corporations are criticized for their tendency to concentrate research and development activities and high technology manufacturing in a few parent countries and to relegate only unskilled or low value-added operations to their foreign subsidiaries. A consequence may be to retard technological and other skills in the host countries. Developed countries, too, tend to worry about becoming satellite "branch plant" economies.

A related issue in the Third World and between countries is the technological gap, which is usually taken to mean the production of technology in two or more countries or differentials in the usage of technology. It can be argued that no gap as such really exists, only a lag between countries, whether developed or developing, and industries. The international transfer and diffusion of knowledge and technology serves to close such gaps.

The so-called brain drain is related to the above issues. It is a name assigned to the migration of highly trained people, such as engineers, scientists, and other professionals, from Third World developing countries to developed countries. Better scientific facilities and all-around opportunities serve to attract such talented people to developed countries. It is not clear that the movement of human capital always has adverse effects on the country losing such capital. For instance, the talented person may not have the opportunity to fully develop and contribute his or her talents in the country of birth. As a result, the world could be the loser.

A country's written and unwritten laws and legal framework are an important aspect of its culture, for they are an important factor in promoting or retarding its development. In many respects, it is through a country's laws that useful insights may be gained into its attitudes, and related issues, see "Legislating Languages: Will It Work?" *Wall Street Journal* (March 13, 1973), p. 13.

14. See Vern Terpstra, *The Cultural Environment of International Business* (Cincinnati: South-Western, 1978), pp. 56–57.

15. Terpstra, *International Business*, pp. 33–37.

16. Robert Slater, *World Religions and World Community* (New York: Columbia University Press, 1968).

17. Gunnar Myrdal discusses the role of cattle in the Indian economy and the largely negative role of the prohibition against their slaughter as one among many other obstructions in the economy. Most writers, including Max Weber, conclude that Hinduism has an overall negative effect on the economy. *Asian Drama: An Inquiry into the Poverty of Nations* (New York: Twentieth Century Fund, 1968).

18. D. K. Rangnekar, *Poverty and Capital Development in India: Contemporary Investment Patterns, Problems, and Planning* (London: Oxford University Press, 1958), p. 81.

19. For a study of the impact of Buddhism on economic development, see Robert C. Lester, *Theravada Buddhism in Southeast Asia* (Ann Arbor: University of Michigan Press, 1972).

20. Myrdal, *Asian Drama*, p. 73.

21. For a useful discussion, see Vera M. Dean, *The Nature of the Non-Western World* (New York: Mentor Books, 1956).

22. See Branimir M. Jankovic, *Medjunarodno javno pravo* (International public law) (Belgrade: Naucna knjiga, 1970).

its "fitness," and if you interpret "fitness" to mean "number of progeny in the next generation," and, finally, if you let "next generations" mean "next tournament," then what you get is that each tournament's results determine the environment of the next tournament. This type of iterated tournament is called ecological because it stimulates ecological adaptation, the shifting of a fixed set of species' populations according to their mutually defined and dynamically developing environment, as contrasted with the mutation-oriented aspects of evolution, where new species can come into existence.

Carrying the ecological tournament generation after generation results in gradual change in the environment. At the start, poor and good programs are equally represented. As the tournament goes on, the poorer programs drop out while the good ones remain. The rank order of the good ones will now change since the field of competitors has changed.

In short, success breeds success only if the successful programs are permitted to interact. If, in contrast, the success of some programs is due mostly to their ability to exploit less successful programs, then as these exploitation-prone programs are gradually squeezed out, the exploiter's base of support is eroded, and the exploiter too will fall out. As Axelrod points out, playing with rules that do not score well is eventually self-defeating. Not being nice may look promising at the start, but in the long run its effect is to destroy the very environment upon which its success depends.

Consider now the ongoing dialogue between developed and developing countries against our theory of cooperation outlined above. Cooperation based on reciprocity can gain a foothold through at least two different mechanisms. One is "kinship," or closely related individuals or institutions. Banks and the debtor/creditor relationship of about $1.3 trillion between developing and developed nations constitute such a relationship.

A second mechanism to overcome a strategy of total defection (ALL D) is for the mutant strategy, cooperation, to arrive in such a cluster so as to provide a nontrivial proportion of the interaction each has. In addition to the $1.3 trillion debt/credit relationship between developing and developed nations, the extensive trade relations that now make for increasing world interdependence provide such a cluster.

As reported by Axelrod and Hamilton, a computer tournament approach will demonstrate that a strategy of TIT-FOR-TAT will fare better than alternative strategies. It is robust. It does well in a variety effects, however, may be the real costs when one's own single defection turns into unending mutual recriminations. In effect, many of the rules actually wind up punishing themselves. The other player simply serves as a mechanism to delay the self-punishment by a few moves.

In essence, there is much to be learned about coping in an environment of mutual power. Indeed, Axelrod reports that many expert strategists from economics, political science, mathematics, sociology, and psychology made the systematic error of being too competitive for their own good, not forgiving enough and too pessimistic about the responsiveness of the other side.

In a non-zero-sum world, a nation does not have to do better than another player nation to do well for itself. The more player nations are interacting, the better. As long as A does well, it is all right if the others do as well or a little better. It is pointless for A to be envious of the success of another country, because in an iterated Prisoner's Dilemma of long duration, the success of the other is virtually a prerequisite of A's doing well for itself.

Clearly this principle holds for our debtor and creditor countries. A country that borrows from another can expect that the loan will be mutually beneficial. There is no point in the borrower's being envious of the creditor's terms and interest. Any attempt to reduce it through an uncooperative practice, such as not making interest and principal payments on time or as agreed, will only encourage the creditor to take retaliatory action. Retaliatory action could take many forms, often without being explicitly labeled as punishment—poorer credit ratings, less prompt deliveries of needed materials, fewer discounts, and, in general, less favorable market conditions for the debtor country's goods and services. In short, the retaliation could make the envy quite expensive. Instead of worrying about the relative profits of the creditor, the debtor should worry about whether another borrowing strategy would be better. For instance, it can lift domestic restrictions on interest paid on savings and bank deposits, thereby mobilizing greater domestic savings, which would reduce external borrowing requirements.

The significance of the environment for the endogenous evolution of institutions à la Hayek is evident in the results reported by Axelrod and others in the "ecological tournament."[6] The tournament consists not only of single subjunctive replay but also of our entire cascade of hypothetical replays, each one's environment determined by the preceding replay. In particular, if you take a program's score in a tournament as a measure of

4 Domestic Constraints in Creditor Countries

CAUSE FOR CONCERN?

Debt, deficits, and stability issues place formidable domestic constraints on the willingness, if not the ability, of creditor countries to be more forthcoming in their dealings with debtor countries. Creditor countries confronted by their own internal deficit and debt problems may well view the problems of debtor countries and proposed solutions as of secondary priority to their own needs. This is understandable. Such consideration, unfortunately, may serve to limit the extension of our cooperation theory.

However, economists are not unanimous in their assessment of a country's debt and deficits. It is a matter of improper bookkeeping for some—a matter of serious concern—and for others an opportunity to restrict and constrain government expenditures and government role in the economy.[1]

The fact is that the importance of debt and deficits depends very much on the circumstances in the country and the disposition of various economists. Debt and deficits are opposed by economists and others who adopt a neoclassical view of deficits. Briefly, if the U.S. economy is considered as a closed economy, persistent deficits will raise interest rates and lower investment. On the other hand, if the U.S. economy is considered as a small open economy, persistent deficits will have the effect of leaving real interest rates and investment unchanged, but the drop in national saving would be financed by higher foreign borrowing achieved by a rise in the foreign value of the dollar and decline in U.S. exports. In either case, net national saving falls, and consumption rises at the expense of some combination of investment and net exports. At present, the net effect is that the United States will enjoy higher living standards—but a lower standard of living in the future compared with the situation if there were no deficits.[2]

From the Keynesian perspective, the view is that U.S. federal deficits are probably overstated in the national income accounts.[3] Deficits can stimulate more unemployment, consumption, and investment through a Keynesian expansion. Another view, the so-called Ricardian equivalence proposition—drawing on the nineteenth-century economist David Ricardo—is that increases in private spending will effectively neutralize federal budget deficits.[4] Yet another view is that any attempts to reduce the size of the deficit by raising taxes will simply lead to more government expenditure and in the long run an expansion in the government sector.[5]

The debt and deficits issue, along with emphasis on fiscal policy, emerged as a response to the practical and theoretical problems of the 1930s. Before that decade, the maximum of sound government finance had been the balanced budget, balanced annually. This rule was coupled with another—a sound money system, which meant the gold standard—and a central banking system that confined itself to maintaining a supply of money sufficient for the legitimate "needs of trade."

The Great Depression cast into prominence ideas advanced by John Maynard Keynes. He postulated that consumers decide to spend or save on the basis of their income, while businesses decide to spend or invest depending on how strong they expect consumer demand will be. A government then could pump up the economy by cutting taxes and increasing spending or could curb the economy by raising taxes; deficits incurred when stimulating the economy were not considered critical. By the end of World War II, Keynes's ideas had won widespread acceptance.

The attitude toward deficits changed again in the late 1970s. Many people now, as in the predepression years, have restored the disciplinary role of deficits. For their part, some economists worried about the link between deficits and the presumed decline in American savings. Other economists criticized the growing government debt for competing with the private sector for consumer savings, thereby driving up interest rates. Higher interest rates, in their view, would make it more costly for businesses to borrow money for capital investment, leading to lower investment and economic stagnation. For its part, government might print more money to pay off some of the debt, which could result in inflation. Thus, the stage was set for a political debate on whether the debt and deficits were little better than a prescription for disaster.

Evidence from the early 1980s records a period in the U.S. economy of mounting government debt and deficits and also indicates low inflation and high output and employment. The record does indicate that the national debt in the U.S. is a somewhat higher percentage of the gross national product than it is in Japan, France, or West Germany, but lower than in Great Britain. Pressure on U.S. interest rates has been relieved by foreign investment in the country, which has risen to more than 3 percent of the gross national product. Such evidence serves to support the view that the $2.7 trillion U.S. debt, important though it is, does not herald a disaster.

More economists are concerned with what is perceived to be a decline in American savings, which fell to about 3 percent of personal disposable income in 1987 from an average of more than 7 percent for the period 1950 to 1980. To be sure, there is at issue the question of how personal savings are to be measured. If the net worth of households is to be included—as some economists prefer—rather than simply personal savings accounts, the figure is much more impressive, averaging about 10 percent of the gross national product during the latter 1980s.

There is also concern that the size of the U.S. debt may well be exaggerated by what the government includes or leaves out of its computation. It is probably a good idea to adjust each annual deficit for inflation in order to measure the debt's real value. Reality would also be better served by adding the budget surpluses of state and local governments to the federal accounts. The state and local levels of government have saved about 9 percent of their annual receipts since 1980.

To all of this may be added the troubling question of whether national accounts can distinguish between government "consumption" and "investment." Critics of existing national accounts argue that the level of investment may be several times the level reported in these accounts. This is a particularly important point, since debt critics hold that government expenditures absorb funds that would otherwise finance capital investment. For this reason, it is suggested that the government's investment spending be separated from its debt bill.

Some ideas for sorting out U.S. government consumption and investment expenditures include revising national accounts, making adjustments for state and local government budgets, and valuing such federal capital assets as universal rights and oil rights. Undoubtedly, such adjustments would reduce the level of existing U.S. debt. In essence, the point is to differentiate those expenditures that are strictly "consumption" from those that are "investment" when attempts are made to reduce debt. Such a separation ultimately will be a political decision resting with politicians and the electorate.[6] As we have noted, the importance of debt and deficits to a country depends on the circumstances it may find itself in.

THE ISSUE OF STABILIZATION POLICIES

This inability to forecast accurately has serious implications for stabilization policies. Together with variability of leads and lags in such policies, erroneous forecasts have pushed some policymakers to reject short-run stabilization policies altogether in favor of a policy of rules.

Finding a strong empirical relationship between several measures of money and economic activity suggests that monetary policy can play a singularly important role in stabilization policy. Indeed, failure to recognize these relationships can have serious consequences for economic activity. These relationships to economic activity, moreover, appear more certain than fiscal actions.

Furthermore, the evidence provided in a number of Federal Reserve Bank of St. Louis Studies is consistent with other evidence that suggests that the money stock is an important indicator of the total thrust of stabilization actions, both monetary and fiscal. In the first instance, changes in the money stock reflect principally discretionary actions of the Federal Reserve System as it uses open market operations, discount rate changes, and reserve requirements. Secondly, the money stock reflects the joint action of the Treasury and Federal Reserve System in financing newly created government debt. These actions are based, in the final analysis, on decisions regarding the monetization of new debt by Federal Reserve actions and on Treasury decisions on changes in its balances at Reserve banks. Thus, changes in government spending financed by monetary expansion are reflected in changes in the monetary base and the money supply.

Many economists argue that the major influence of fiscal actions results only if expenditures are financed by monetary expansion. In the United States, the Federal Reserve does not buy securities from the government. Its open market operations, along with other actions, serve to provide funds in the markets in which both the government and private individuals borrow.

Moreover, it is not easy to reverse a stimulative stance in fiscal policy—a result, in part, of the institutional context in which fiscal tools are used. A part of these fiscal tools, such as automatic stabilizers, can be redirected very quickly. These programs expand and contract more or less automatically in response to changes in the pace that the economy is expanding. Such programs include unemployment compensation, welfare programs, leasing subsidies, and, in the United States, the progressive nature of the federal tax structure.

Some insight into how difficult it is to quickly change the posture of fiscal policy in either direction may be had by considering that all the programs in the United States require congressional approval.[7] This approval must be in a form that provides for the actions sought by the administration. Bills are sometimes changed in committee or on the floor of Congress in ways that significantly redirect their thrusts.

Much the same is true in tax legislation; political realities often intervene to make either raising or lowering taxes a long, drawn-out process. The political give-and-take may very well result in a less than optimal tax system.

Transfer payments, although outlays rather than taxes, are subject to the same sort of forces that slow tax changes and to considerable temptation to embellish a proposed program. In fact, once recipients become accustomed to the payments, they and their political representatives will not be anxious to see them withdrawn when the need for stimulus passes. Discretionary changes in transfer payments tend to be one-way stabilization tools at best, for use when a stimulus is needed.

J. de Larosiere, director of the International Monetary Fund, argued forcefully in March 1982 that the "fiscal policy followed by many countries over the past decade has been the basic ingredient for stagflation. Rather than being the 'stabilizing factor,' as advocated by Keynes, fiscal policy has become one of the major destabilizing forces in many countries.[8] He underscores that many of these transfer programs and other benefits were introduced when their cost was low and their future fiscal consequences were ignored. In other cases, highly optimistic forecasts about important variables such as growth, unemployment, and inflation were made at the same time the programs were introduced or expanded during the 1960s and early 1970s. Changed circumstances in the 1970s made it very difficult for many countries to keep their commitments and still pursue a sound fiscal policy.

Readily available data suggest the impact of these developments on public expenditure for seven major industrial countries.[9] For these countries, the ratio of total public expenditure to gross domestic product (GDP) rose from 29 percent in 1965 to around 37 percent in recent years. For some individual countries, these increases have been even more pronounced. In Canada, West Germany, Italy, Japan, Spain, and Great Britain, the ratio of total public expenditure to GDP rose by more than 10 percentage points between 1965 and the end of the 1970s. For some of the smaller industrial countries, such as Belgium, Ireland, Luxembourg, the Netherlands, Norway, Portugal, and Sweden, the increases were even more pronounced, exceeding 15 percentage points. In all of these countries, including France, the ratio of public expenditure to GDP now exceeds 40 percent. In all cases, concludes de Larosiere, entitlement programs and other transfers have been the main factor in this expansion.

A MONETARY AND FISCAL POLICY MIX

How should monetary and fiscal policy be mixed? Milton Friedman discussed this issue at some length during the height of the Korean War in 1951.[10] This, too, was a period of military buildup in the United States that pushed inflation into double digits.

Friedman argues that "monetary and fiscal measures are the only appropriate means of controlling inflation." He rules out any recourse to wage-price controls. According to Friedman, monetary and fiscal measures are substitutes within a wide range of options. A large budget surplus would be consistent with no inflation, or, for that matter, any degree of inflation.

7 The Debt Burden and World Monetary Stability

IN RETROSPECT

The story of the growth in Third World debt is a complex one indeed, as we have underscored in our study. Its outline is plain enough; as a group, developing countries switched from sources of borrowing from governments—largely at fixed interest accounting for most of the growth in debt.

The decision by the leading debtor countries to borrow from banks has forced them into three types of difficulties. The first is excessive reliance on short-term credit, particularly into the short-term interbank market. These credits are callable and can vanish overnight. A borrowing country must replace them with conventional bank loans, thereby making its rescheduling problems all the more difficult.

The second difficulty has been the high cost of loans. To be sure, countries like Yugoslavia, Mexico, Brazil, and other leading debtors were sensible to borrow heavily at variable rates in the 1970s. If the world economy boomed, interest rates would rise—but then so would their exports; if it slumped, then interest rates and exports would both fall, as well. What created a problem for borrowers was a combination of rising interest rates and falling export earnings. According to the debtors, this was something they could not have forecast.

Unfortunately for the debtor argument, nothing in economic analysis argues persuasively that interest rates and export earnings rise and fall together. They moved against each other in 1976 and 1977, favorably to the borrowers because dollar interest rates fell while their export earnings rose. That should have suggested to the debtor countries that an unfavorable combination is possible.

Indeed, this is what happened in 1980–82, with disastrous consequences to the debtor countries. Having built up so much variable-rate debt, many of these countries had lost the flexibility they needed to cope with a world recession. As a group, the Third World had used 13.5 percent of its exports to service its debt in 1970; by 1980, the ratio was still only 13.6 percent. By 1982 it had risen sharply to 20.7 percent, and several of the biggest Latin American borrowers faced debt-service ratios of more than 100 percent.

The third difficulty turns on the front loading of repayments, in good part the result of high nominal interest rates. Indeed, one of the more important consequences of inflation is its effect on interest rates and what these rates then do to the repayment burden of the borrower. Lenders know that inflation will reduce the real value of their capital, so they demand compensation in the form of higher interest rates. A 5 percent interest rate on a ten-year loan of $100 would, in a noninflationary world, involve a first-year repayment of $15 ($5 interest and $10 amortization). However, with inflation at 10 percent, and supposing interest rates rise to 15 percent, the borrower has to pay $25 ($15 interest and $10 amortization) in year one. In effect, to compensate the lender for a 10 percent fall in the value of his capital, the borrower has to pay 67 percent more in the first year than he would have paid had there been no inflation.

This is not a one-sided phenomenon, and borrowers reap an advantage as inflation shrinks the real value of the capital repayments. In the 1970s, front loading began to be applied to development finance in a new fashion. Even assuming that Third World countries were putting their bank loans to profitable use, no development project starts generating big money in the first year. The net result was that the Third World borrowers and their banker-creditors were caught in an impossible situation.

The solution is not through indexation, as suggested by some and quite properly taken to task by others. Thus, if borrowers had agreed to pay an interest rate of 5 percent plus the real value of the $100 loan in ten annual installments, their bill would have been only $16.50 ($11 for amortizing one-tenth of the revalued $100 loan plus $5.50 in interest on $100); their situation could certainly be more manageable. The difficulty with such an indexation arrangement is that indexed loans would require indexed deposits because no bank could mismatch its assets and liabilities. If banks started indexing their foreign loans, they would be under pressure to do the same domestically.

Once started, indexing in banking would spread through the economy. For various reasons, some governments in the 1970s declined indexation as a policy. As a result of simple calculation, serious problems would have been ahead for the Third World debtor countries unless interest rates declined sharply and debtor country export earnings increased significantly; neither happened.

As a result, during the early stages of the 1980–82 disinflation, countries found that they were increasing their borrowing but getting less spendable capital—interest rate payments were absorbing a larger share of the total. The Mexican near-default in August 1982 shocked the governments of the industrial creditor countries into treating the Third World's debt problems much more seriously than they had been disposed to do earlier.

As we have discussed, help and treatment for Third World debt problems have several approaches. One is emergency loans of some kind from the Bank for International Settlements (BIS) and other world organizations. Another is thorough rescheduling of bank debt so that borrowers are relieved of paying capital in the short term, over the objection of the smaller creditor banks. The larger banks, knowing that they have no option but to reschedule, have charged exorbitant fees for the service and have widened their spreads. A third is more money and an expanded role for the IMF. A fourth is the relaxation of monetary policy in industrial countries in the hope that interest rates would fall and stimulate recovery. It is this issue that we now consider.

PROVIDING FOR WORLD MONETARY STABILITY: MONETARY POLICY

The Third World debt crisis has had an all-too-real effect. Central banks have eased their monetary policies to accommodate the Third World debtor countries. This has also increased uncertainty about the future course of world inflation and has helped to keep interest rates up. It is easy to see how the world economy could get caught in a vicious circle of slow growth, each turn making the Third World's debt less financeable without cutting imports further, with each one reducing growth in the industrial creditor countries. The consequences for people in every country would be grim; for those in the poorest countries, the prognosis would be the most grim. The surest, perhaps the only, way to escape such a circle is through the preservation of worldwide monetary stability, especially in the major industrial countries. This is a manageable task.

Policy recommendations are forthcoming from several quarters. Control of the stock of money and thus of inflation prompts monetarists and others to support the use of monetary policy. Monetarists also tend to favor greater reliance on monetary rather than fiscal policy because of the nondiscriminatory consequences of monetary restraint. Objections to monetary policy come mainly from Keynesians, who tend to opt for fiscal policy as a means to stabilize the economy.[1] Other critics of monetary policy are also found in groups who believe themselves injured by its operation.

The usefulness of the tool of monetary policy depends very much on the skill with which it is applied, as well as on its effectiveness. Monetary policy as a tool could be highly effective but poorly administered. Alternatively it could have limited effectiveness but be well operated.

The general evidence points to monetary policy as the cause for high interest rates. It is in the conduct of monetary policy by central banks that the principal culprit for high interest rates is to be found. In the world's leading economy, the Federal Reserve's conduct of monetary policy is responsible for high U.S. interest rates. The volatile movements in money supply growth make prediction of the direction of monetary policy impossible and create doubts in the financial markets about the Federal Reserve's willingness or ability to meet its targets. During the critical years of the world recession (1981–82), short-term interest rates were kept high during months when money supply growth was too slow to meet the needs of trade, and inflation expectations revived during months when money supply growth exploded, adding the inflation premium to interest rates.

According to some economists, not only is monetary policy responsible for high interest rates but, in the United States, it is also responsible for the budget deficit. Thus, monetary policy that restricts the growth of investment and GNP also increases government deficit. The slower growth of national income depresses tax revenues; these large deficits then build up the public debt faster, increasing future net interest expenses. Monetary restraint may increase real interest rates, contributing further to net interest expenses.

Recent economic research suggests that it is the Federal Reserve System, not former President Reagan's tax cut, that is responsible for the 1979–82 recession. Statistical comparisons show that the 1981–82 deceleration in U.S. monetary growth is of greater magnitude and longer duration than during any comparable period since 1960. With the tax cut delayed, there was no appropriate fiscal policy in place to offset the adverse effects of extraordinarily tight money on the economy. The tax cuts were not initiated early enough to moderate the effects of restraint in money supply growth. Recession and large U.S. budget deficits were inevitable.

More and more, economists are coming to the view that the Federal Reserve should deal with the deficit by letting the American economy grow and not base its policy on unsubstantiated fears of crowding out. In effect, a new logic seems to be displacing the old wisdom: Deficits must either crowd out investment by raising interest rates or be monetized by the Federal Reserve, adding to inflation and leading ultimately to higher interest rates.

GOALS, OBJECTIVES, AND CRITICISM OF MONETARY POLICY

Discussions of monetary policy as a tool of general economic stability often focus on its speed and effectiveness of action. Its great virtue, argue some of its supporters, is that monetary policy can be altered quickly and adjusted finely to changing circumstances. Critics contend that monetary policy as conducted in practice is slow to adjust to changes in the economic environment and may, therefore, aggravate the economic instability that it seeks to mitigate.

The management of money has had a long history. Monetary policy has varied in instruments used, in stated objectives, and in the economic philosophy of policymakers. Central bankers and others often cite Bagehot's nineteenth-century dictum that "money will not manage itself" as justification for central bank intervention in the economy. Collapse of the international monetary and financial structure in the

Great Depression cast doubt on the ability of central banks to effectively manage money. Indeed, by the late 1930s, fiscal policy or the planned balance of Treasury receipts and expenditures became a more powerful economic factor than monetary policy. In fact, during World War II, the U.S. Federal Reserve mainly played the role of interest-rate stabilizer and guarantor of Treasury financing.

Keynesian ideas and influence, as well as the example of World War II, underscored the effectiveness of fiscal policy. Large government spending financed by large deficits shifted the balance in the U.S. economy from unemployment to a labor shortage. Moreover, the standard of living of the civilian population was preserved, while at the same time the country fought a world war. Then it is little wonder that the Employment Act of 1946 put almost sole stress on the use of fiscal policy.

Monetary policy in the postwar era served to stabilize interest rates until it broke free with the Federal Reserve and Treasury agreement in March 1951. Even after the break, however, monetary policy was expected to primarily support interest rates. Essentially, an increased supply of bank reserves was expected to lower the cost and increase the availability of credit. The cost and availability of credit was then expected to stimulate business and consumers to larger investment spending. It was soon realized that this stimulative action would have some inflationary impact. The matter was presented as a trade-off. How much inflation should be tolerated in return for an increase in employment and economic activity?

For almost two decades, matters seemed to be going well as monetary and fiscal policy management stabilized the economy. To be sure, recession and economic dislocations occurred, but they were considered minor departures from the otherwise successful performance of the economy. Nevertheless, criticism of monetary and fiscal policy, especially the execution of such policies, has been a source of academic criticism extending to policymaking areas.

Monetarism is in the forefront of such criticism. Its primary idea that money is the central causative economic factor in prices and economic activity, while not new, received significant theoretical, empirical, and historical support in the studies by Milton Friedman and those of his followers.[2] Other important results obtained in these studies is that there is a significant and variable lag between stimulative monetary policy and its economic benefits. The length of this lag is estimated at anywhere from six months to more than two years. These results are confirmed for other countries as well. Given the length and variability of the lag, the effects of monetary policy appear long after they are no longer appropriate. As a result, discretionary monetary policy may have a destabilizing effect on the economy.

The monetarist recommendation is to adjust the money supply to grow at the same rate as the potential for real economic output. There is no need for discretionary monetary policy and management.

These ideas are not new. What is new is that monetarist ideas have reached policy levels hitherto unattainable by earlier proponents of similar ideas. There are indications that various central banks appear to shape their policies now more in terms of monetary magnitudes than earlier, even though discretionary monetary policy is retained.

The attack on discretionary monetary policy is closely supported by people promoting the idea of "rational expectations."[3] Essentially, the idea is that labor groups and investors will correctly anticipate the inflationary impact of stimulative government policies—monetary and fiscal—and take self-protective measures that will thwart the stimulative policies. Labor will seek higher wages to offset expected inflation. Investors will seek higher interest rates for the same reason. Higher wages and higher interest rates will make investment unattractive, so stimulative action will not produce the desired results. We shall have inflation but not the trade-off in increased output.

Given the logic of these ideas, well known in the central banking establishment, does discretionary monetary policy have a future? Apart from technological unemployment among central bankers and their understandable hesitancy to be so displaced, there are other reasons that discretionary policy may continue to have a future. First, the very mechanics of central banking may encourage it. For instance, the reserve supply mechanism is subject to sharp impacts from such sources as Treasury cash management and currency demands, which could be, although unlikely, separated from discretionary monetary management.

Second, Treasury financing in practice encourages discretionary monetary policy. Although it is possible to separate Treasury financing from dependence on central bank support, as occurred in the United States before World War I, it is not likely that ministers of finance or secretaries of treasury would venture into contemporary financial markets to meet vast government fund requirements without central bank support. Finally, public perception of monetary affairs cultivates the belief that central banks do control interest rates.

New ideas are having an important impact in the form of a monetary policy that is less variable in its nature. The amplitude of changes in the character of monetary policy is likely to be less than in the past. The rhetoric and observation, if not practice, appear to suggest this. For instance, on October 6, 1979, the Federal Reserve announced the beginning of a new approach to the implementation of monetary policy: It would attempt to achieve better control of the growth of monetary aggregates by "placing greater emphasis in day-to-day operations on the supply of bank reserves and less emphasis on confining short-term fluctuations in the federal funds rate."[4] So much for the rhetoric. In practice, over the year 1980, the Federal Reserve did not achieve the degree of declaration in M1B and M2 money growth rates that it had announced as its objective for the year.[5] According to observers, experience with the reserve targeting procedures does not support the view that fluctuations in the money supply in 1980 reflect problems with monetary control that are basic to the operating procedure. Under the reserve targeting procedure, short-term monetary control may be improved in future years.

Much the same is true in other industrial countries. For example, in Great Britain the Thatcher government has stuck closely to several principles of monetary policy initiated under the Labor government.[6] These include the following: (1) formal targets for monetary growth, which were first adopted in 1976 (they are expressed as a range rather than a single number, recognizing that precise control is impossible); (2) the definition of the target as a single measure of this (sterling M3) money supply; and (3) the employment since 1978 of a "rolling target"; although it applies to the next twelve months, it is reviewed every six months. In practice, monetary control in Great Britain has been difficult to achieve. Overshooting targets has become the norm. The reasons targets are missed vary from year to year, a fact that appears to be consistent with "Goodhart's Law" (coined by C. Goodhart, chief monetary advisor to the Bank of England), which states that any measure of the money supply that is officially controlled promptly loses its meaning.[7]

Few will quibble with the idea that monetary policy ought to foster economic growth. The less developed countries in Africa, Asia, and Latin America have many characteristics in common, including a relatively undiversified and inelastic productive system that responds only slowly to demand activated by an expansionary monetary policy. In these countries a thin line exists between inflation and the loss of international reserves on the one hand and a slow rate of growth on the other. However, within these limits, monetary policy does play an important role.

In many developing countries, demand by borrowers for credit tends to be insensitive to small changes in interest rates. An alternative to pushing interest rates to exorbitant levels is, according to some, to resort to direct allocation of credit. Unfortunately, such action typically implies the imposition of direct controls. These controls tend to be discriminatory, personal, and contrary to the principles of an open and flexible market economy.

As an instrument of monetary policy, open market operations are not effective in developing countries because of the absence of an adequate securities market. Rediscount policy may be effective in those countries where banks are accustomed to borrowing from the central bank. It is also used in many countries to influence and guide the flow of credit to "desired ends." A central bank may grant favorable treatment or it may limit rediscounts to the refinancing of certain types of loans, encouraging banks to lend for these purposes.

Changes in reserve requirements may also prove effective. However, in many of the developing countries, liquidity ratios tend to be stable, and in some the purpose of changes in reserve requirements appears to be to direct credit toward certain users by recognizing their debt instruments as liquid assets.

WHAT ARE THE PROSPECTS?

World free traders want the developing countries to grow to better serve the Third World's own needs and to lubricate the trading system. The debt collectors, on the other hand, want the Third World to keep tightening its belt and run huge export surpluses, the better to pay back its debts. Moreover, even though it is recognized that trade and debt are intimately linked, they are subject to distinct international bureaucracies and different ministries or cabinet departments in each country. These are indeed contradictory signals, which must be clarified if the world is to approach a satisfactory resolution of the debt while at the same time avoiding monetary uncertainty and instability.

One influential official in the world's bureaucracy who straddled both the trade and debt issues is former U.S. treasury secretary, later secretary of state, James A. Baker III. In 1985 he proposed that the World Bank and the world's commercial banks supply additional credit to the developing countries to help them out of the austerity trap. But, as New Jersey Senator Bill Bradley observed, the Baker initiative would only put the Third World deeper in debt. Bradley proposed not only new credits but also refinancing old debt at lower interest rates and some forgiveness of principal. It may well be that while Baker has the right impulse, Bradley has the more appropriate plan.

We should keep clearly in mind that arguments calling for the growing mutual dependence among members of the global economy and the virtues of free trade should also include the Third World countries. Belt tightening in Third World debtor countries means empty stomachs not only in a Third World barrio but also in many an industry in the developed creditor countries.

If the trade system fails, it will not be because the United States, Japan, and the European community could not agree on how to divide the trilateral spoils but very likely because rich countries exacted too heavy a price on the poor ones.

The Third World debt is indeed a singular threat to monetary stability in the world's liberal interdependent trading system. Although the major industrial countries claim they want to dismantle trade barriers and promote growth, the austerity now being inflicted on the Third World stimulates the worst sort of mercantilism at the expense of the world economy as a whole.

Although tariffs have been progressively reduced over the years, whole sectors of the global economy are outside the jurisdiction of the General Agreement on Tariffs and Trade (GATT). Autos, textiles, steel, aircraft, and electronics are subject to a tangle of subsidies, quotas, industrial policies, and other breaches of free trade. For instance, agriculture, which was never part of GATT in 1986, was subsidized at up to $40 billion annually in the United States and Europe.

Efforts to dismantle trade barriers and promote growth are simply not aided by the insistence of the IMF and world bankers that Third World debtors close their home markets to imports while accelerating their exports to the industrialized nations to earn hard currency for debt repayment.

In the late 1970s, the Third World was growing at a good rate, financed by capital—mostly bank loans—from the United States and Europe. The Third World countries were the fastest-growing market for the exports of industrialized countries.

Since 1981, however, as the austerity programs have been put into place, the world's poor countries have dried up as markets. According to GATT estimates, the world's sixteen most heavily indebted poor countries in 1981 imported $20 billion more than they exported. In 1984 and 1985, they ran a net trade surplus of nearly $30 billion. Although that sounds like salutory belt tightening, it is, in fact, self-defeating, because they achieved those surpluses by shrinking their own economies and importing less, not by exporting more. Responses such as these reduce the debt-servicing capacity of the developing countries, damage their potential for economic and social growth, and restrict the export opportunities of their partners.

There are contradictory priorities between those who want the developing countries to grow so as to better serve the interdependent global trading system and those who want the Third World to keep tightening its belt and run huge export surpluses the better to pay back its debt. Until these contradictory priorities are satisfactorily resolved, prospects for debtor and creditor countries alike leave much to be desired.

Indeed, by the end of the 1980s, austerity measures imposed on the poorest countries by the International Monetary Fund as a condition for new loans had produced few positive results. "I guess you could say the sacrifices have been in vain," said Roger Lawrence, an official of the United Nations Conference on Trade and Development, in referring to the reductions in social spending and the drop in living standards that the austerity measures have caused.[8] According to the UN report, the economies of the developing countries of Africa and Latin America have stagnated or worsened. The report points to their large foreign debts as the cause of their poor performance.

In its review of the IMF adjustment programs, the UN examined forty-two nations with a combined population of more than 400 million and with low per capita income levels. The report found that of the twelve least-developed countries that have applied for IMF austerity adjustment programs for most of the 1980s, the growth rates of only three—Bangladesh, Gambia, and Mali—were above the average for all the least-developed countries. The main result of the IMF austerity programs, which focus on cutting public spending, devaluing the national currency to stimulate exports, and reducing imports, has been a contraction of economic activity. The report's recommendation "is increased debt relief, more flexible adjustment programs, and better access to industrialized countries import markets."[9]

For its part, the IMF in its 1989 annual report recorded that as of April 1989, 11 members of a total membership of 151 countries had $3 billion of IMF debts overdue longer than six months, compared with 9 members with overdue obligations of $2.2 billion a year earlier. The report is that world prosperity was endangered by high debt and lagging investment in many debtor countries.[10]

The debt arrears problem is particularly critical for the IMF because the resultant squeeze on its liquid cash reserves comes at a time when it is being called upon to play an increasingly active role in the formulation of a strategy to deal with Third World debt, which we discussed elsewhere. The rise in arrears is considered unusual because the IMF holds preferred-creditor status, which means it must be paid ahead of other lenders to the Third World except for the World Bank. In most cases, the nonpayment reflects the growing difficulties of debtor developing countries in trying to cope with the crushing debt burdens that have weighed on the global economy since 1982.

NOTES

1. James Tobin, "Friedman's Theoretical Framework," *Journal of Political Economy* (September–October 1972), pp. 852–63; Warren L. Smith, "Neo-Keynesian View of Monetary Policy," *Controlling Monetary Aggregates*, Federal Reserve Bank of Boston (June 1969), pp. 105–26; Ronald L. Teigen, "A Critical Look at Monetarist Economics," *Review*, Federal Reserve Bank of St. Louis (January 1972), pp. 10–25; A. S. Flinder and R. M. Solow, "Does Fiscal Policy Matter?" *Journal of Public Economics* (November 1973), pp. 319–37; James Tobin and Willem Buiter, "Long-Run Effects of Fiscal and Monetary Policy on Aggregate Demand," Lowes Foundation Discussion Paper No. 384 (December 13, 1974), in *Essays in Economics*, J. Tobin, ed. (Cambridge, Mass.: M.I.T. Press, 1982), pp. 161–235; John Kenneth Galbraith, *A Life in Our Times* (Boston: Houghton Mifflin, 1981); George Macesich, *The International Monetary Economy and the Third World* (New York: Praeger, 1981); and George Macesich and H. Tsai, *Money in Economic Systems* (New York: Praeger, 1982).

2. For a discussion of the relevant ideas and policy issues in monetarism, see George Macesich, *Politics of Monetarism: Its Historical and Institutional*

Development (Totowa, N.J.: Rowman and Allanheld, 1984); and George Macesich, *Monetarism* (New York: Praeger, 1983). For the relevance of monetarism to Yugoslavia, see Dimitrije Dimitrijevic and George Macesich, *Money and Finance in Yugoslavia: A Comparative Analysis* (New York: Praeger, 1984).

3. George Macesich, *Monetary Policy and Rational Expectations* (New York: Praeger, 1986) and the studies cited.

4. R. Alton Gilbert and Michael E. Trebing, "The FOMC in 1980: A Year of Reserve Targeting," *Review*, Federal Reserve Bank of St. Louis (August–September 1981), pp. 2–22.

5. M1B = (currency + private demand deposits at commercial banks excluding deposits due to foreign commercial banks and official institutions + other checkable deposits, e.g., negotiable-order of withdrawal accounts, automatic transfer service accounts, credit union share drafts, and demand deposits at mutual savings banks).

M2 = M1B + savings and small-denomination time deposits of all depository institutions, shares in money market mutual funds, and overnight Eurodollar deposits held by U.S. residents at Caribbean branches of U.S. banks. Gilbert and Trebing, "FOMC in 1980," pp. 5 and 16; Thomas D. Simpson, "The Redefined Monetary Aggregates," *Federal Reserve Bulletin* (February 1980), p. 100; *Improving Monetary Statistics* (Washington, D.C.: Board of Governors of the Federal Reserve System, 1978).

6. *The Economist* (November 14, 1981), pp. 102–3. The British monetary target since 1978 is defined as sterling M3 = notes and coin circulation + sterling current account held by the British private sector + sterling deposit accounts held by all British residents.

7. *The Economist* (November 14, 1981), p. 103.

8. Burton Bollag, "U.N. Report Faults I.M.F. Austerity Requirements," *New York Times* (September 6, 1989), p. 35.

9. Bollag, "U.N. Report," p. 35.

10. Clyde H. Farnsworth, "Bad Debt Rose Sharply at I.M.F. Last Year," *New York Times* (September 15, 1989), p. 30.

Bibliography

Axelrod, Robert. *Evolution of Cooperation*. New York: Basic Books, 1984.

Axelrod, Robert, and Douglas Dion. "The Further Evolution of Cooperation." *Science* (December 9, 1988), pp. 1385–1389.

Axelrod, Robert, and William D. Hamilton. "The Evolution of Cooperation." *Science* (March 27, 1981), pp. 1390–1396.

Banks, Arthur S., and Robert B. Textor. *A Cross-Policy Survey*. Cambridge: M.I.T. Press, 1953.

Baron, S. W. *Modern Nationalism and Religion*. New York: Harper, 1947.

Barro, Robert J. "Are Government Bonds Net Wealth?" *Journal of Political Economy* (November-December 1974), pp. 1095–1117.

———. "Neoclassical Approach to Fiscal Policy." In *Modern Business Cycle Theory*, Robert J. Barro, ed. Cambridge: Harvard University Press, 1989.

———. "The Ricardian Approach to Budget Deficits." *Journal of Economic Perspectives* (Spring 1989), pp. 54–57.

Becker, Gary S. *The Economics of Discrimination*. Chicago: University of Chicago Press, 1957.

Belassa, B., and R. Nelson, eds. *Economic Progress, Private Values, and Public Policy: Essays in Honor of William Felver*. Amsterdam: North-Holland, 1977.

Bollag, Burton. "U.N. Report Faults I.M.F. Austerity Requirements." *New York Times* (September 6, 1989), p. 35.

Breton, Albert. "The Economics of Nationalism." *Journal of Political Economy*, vol. 72 (1964): pp. 376–86.

Brozen, Yale. "Minimum Wages and Household Workers." *Journal of Law and Economics* (October 1962).

Buchanan, James M. *The Demand and Supply of Public Goods*. Chicago: Rand McNally, 1968.

Buchanan, James M., and Gordon Tullock. *The Calculus of Consent*. Ann Arbor: University of Michigan Press, 1962.

Buchanan, James M., and Richard E. Wagner. *Democracy in Deficit*. New York: Academic Press, 1977.

Cairncross, A. K. *Home and Foreign Investment, 1870–1913*. Cambridge: Cambridge University Press, 1953.

Carr, W. H. *Nationalism and After*. New York: Macmillan, 1945.

Coase, Ronald. "The Problem of Social Cost." *Journal of Law and Economics* (October 1960), pp. 1–45.

Cohen, M, T. Nagel, and T. Scanlon, eds. *War and Moral Responsibility*. Princeton: Princeton University Press, 1974.

Colberg, Marshall R. "Minimum Wage Effects on Florida Economic Development." *Journal of Law and Economics* (October 1960).

Dean, Vera M. *The Nature of the Non-Western World*. New York: Mentor Books, 1956.

Deutsch, Karl Wolfgang. *Nationalism and Social Communication*. Cambridge: MIT Press, 1953.

———. *Nationalism and Social Communication: An Inquiry into the Foundations of Nationality*. New York: Wiley, 1953.

Deutsch, Karl Wolfgang, and W. J. Poltz, eds. *Nation-Building*. New York: Atherton, 1963.

Dimitrijevic, Dimitrije, and George Macesich, *Money and Finance in Yugoslavia: A Comparative Analysis*. New York: Praeger, 1984.

Doob, L. W. *Patriotism and Nationalism: Their Psychological Foundations*. New Haven: Yale University Press, 1964.

Downs, Anthony. *An Economic Theory of Democracy*. New York: Harper, 1957.

Earle, E. M., ed. *Nationalism and Internationalism: Essays Inscribed to Carlton J. A. Hayes*. New York: Columbia University Press, 1950.

Eban, A. *The Tide of Nationalism*. New York: Horizon Press, 1959.

The Economist. (July 30, 1983), p. 61.

———. (November 14, 1981), pp. 102–3.

Eisner, Robert. "Budget Deficits: Rhetoric and Reality." *Journal of Economic Perspectives* (Spring 1989), pp. 73–93.

———. *How Real Is the Federal Deficit?* New York: Free Press, 1986.

European Investment Bank. *Cahiers BEI/EIB Papers* (March 1989), no. 8, pp. 18–21.

Farnsworth, Clyde H. "Bad Debt Rose Sharply at I.M.F. Last Year." *New York Times* (September 6, 1989), p. 30.

Feldstein, Martin S. "Social Security, Induced Retirement, and Aggregate Capital Accumulation." *Journal of Political Economy* (September-October 1974), pp. 905–26.

Flinder, A. S., and R. M. Solow. "Does Fiscal Policy Matter?" *Journal of Public Economics* (November 1973), pp. 319–37.

Friedman, Milton. "Why the Twin Deficits Are a Blessing." *Wall Street Journal* (December 14, 1988), p. A14.

Friedman, Milton, ed. *Essays in Positive Economics*. Chicago: University of Chicago Press, 1953.

Galbraith, John Kenneth. *A Life in Our Times*. Boston: Houghton Mifflin, 1981.

Gewirtz, Carl. "Gambit for Third World Debt Burden: Baker's Plan Linked to Exports." *International Herald Tribune* (June 21, 1989), pp. 11, 15.

Gibbons, H. A. *Nationalism and Internationalism*. New York: Stokes, 1930.

Gilbert, R. Alton, and Michael E. Trebing. "The FOMC in 1980: A Year of Reserve Targeting." *Review*. Federal Reserve Bank of St. Louis (August-September 1981), pp. 2–22.

Gladbe, R., and Dwight R. Lee. *Microeconomics: Theory and Applications*. New York: Harcourt Brace Jovanovich, 1980.

Gooch, G. P. *Nationalism*. New York: Harcourt, Brace, and Howe, 1920.

Gramlich, Edward M. "Budget Deficits and National Savings: Are Politicians Exogenous?" *Journal of Economic Perspectives* (Spring 1989), pp. 23–35.

Hayes, C. J. H. *The Historical Evolution of Modern Nationalism*. New York: R. R. Smith, 1931.

Hertz, F. O. *Nationality in History and Politics*. New York: Oxford University Press, 1944.

Higgins, Benjamin. *Economic Development Past and Present*. New York: Norton, 1968.

Hinsley, F. H. *Nationalism and the International System*. London: Hodder and Straugton, 1973.

Hofstadter, Douglas R. "Metamagical Themas." *Scientific American* (May 1983), pp. 16–26.

Improving Monetary Statistics. Washington, D.C.: Board of Governors of the Federal Reserve System, 1978.

Jankovic, Branimir. *Medjunarodno javno pravo* (International public law). Belgrade: Naucna knjiga, 1970.

Jaszi, O. *The Dissolution of the Habsburg Monarchy*. Chicago: University of Chicago Press, 1929.

Johnson, Harry G., ed. *Economic Nationalism in Old and New States*. Chicago: University of Chicago Press, 1967.

Kahn, A. E. *Great Britain in the World Economy*. New York: Columbia University Press, 1946.

Kohn, Hans. *The Idea of Nationalism*. New York: Macmillan, 1944.

Kuznets, Simon. *Economic Growth and Structure: Selected Essays*. New York: Norton, 1965.

Larosiere, J. de. "Coexistence of Fiscal Deficits, High Tax Burdens Is Consequence of Pressures for Public Spending." *Survey* (March 22, 1982), p. 82.

Lester, Robert C. *Theravada Buddhism in Southeast Asia*. Ann Arbor: University of Michigan Press, 1972.

Luce, D., and H. Raiffa. *Games and Decisions*. New York: Wiley, 1957, pp. 94–102.

Macesich, George. "Are Wage Differentials Resilient? An Empirical Test." *Southern Economic Journal* (April 1961).

———. *Commercial Banking and Regional Development in the United States: 1950–60*. Tallahassee: Florida State University Press, 1963.

———. "Economic Theory and the Austro-Hungarian Ausgleich of 1867." In *Der Österreichischungarische Ausgleich, 1967*, Ludovit Holitik, ed. Bratislava: Slovak Academy, 1971.

———. *Geldpolitik in einem gemeinsamen europäischen Markt*. [Money in a common market setting]. Baden-Baden: Nomos Verlagsgesellschaft, 1972.

———. *The International Monetary Economy and The Third World*. New York: Praeger, 1981.

———. *Monetarism*. New York: Praeger, 1983.

———. *Monetary Policy and Rational Expectations*. New York: Praeger, 1986.

———. *Monetary Reform and Cooperation Theory*. New York: Praeger, 1989.

———. *Politics of Monetarism: Its Historical and Institutional Development*. Totowa, N.J.: Rowman and Allanheld, 1984.

———. "Supply and Demand for Money in Canada." In *Varieties of Monetary Experience*, David Meiselman, ed. Chicago: University of Chicago Press, 1971, pp. 249–96.

———. "The Theory of Economic Integration and the Experience of the Balkan and Danubian Countries before 1914." *Proceedings of the First International Congress on Southeast European Studies*, Sofia, Bulgaria (1966), and *Florida State University Slavic Papers I* (1967).

———. *World Banking and Finance: Cooperation versus Conflict*. New York: Praeger, 1984.

———. *Yugoslavia: The Theory and Practice of Development Planning*. Charlottesville: University Press of Virginia, 1964.

Macesich, George, and Charles T. Stewart, Jr. "Recent Department of Labor Studies of Minimum Wage Effects." *Southern Economic Journal* (April 1960).

Macesich, George, and H. Tsai. *Money in Economic Systems*. New York: Praeger, 1982.

Myrdal, Gunnar. *Asian Drama: An Inquiry into the Poverty of Nations*. New York: Twentieth Century Fund, 1968.

Nayar, B. R. *National Communication and Language Policy in India*. New York: Praeger, 1969.

Peterson, John M. "Recent Needs in Minimum Wage Theory." *Southern Economic Journal* (July 1962).

Rangnekar, D. K. *Poverty and Capital Development in India: Contemporary Investment Patterns, Problems, and Planning*. London: Oxford University Press, 1958.

Rapoport, Anton, and A. M. Chammah. *Prisoner's Dilemma*. Ann Arbor: University of Michigan Press, 1965.

Reynolds, L. G. "Wages and Employment in the Labor-Surplus Economy." *American Economic Review* (March 1965).

Schneider, Louis, and Charles Bonjean, eds. *The Idea of Culture in the Social Sciences*. Cambridge: Cambridge University Press, 1973.

Schotter, Andrew. *The Economic Theory of Social Institutions*. Cambridge: Cambridge University Press, 1981.

Schotter, Andrew, and Gerhard Schwodiauer. "Economics and the Theory of Games: A Survey." *Journal of Economic Literature* (June 1980), pp. 479–527.

Seers, Dudley. *The Political Economy of Nationalism*. Oxford: Oxford University Press, 1983.

Shafer, B. C. *Faces of Nationalism*. New York: Harcourt Brace Jovanovich, 1972.

Simpson, Thomas D. "The Redefined Monetary Aggregates." *Federal Reserve Bulletin* (February 1980), p. 100.

Slater, Robert. *World Religions and World Community*. New York: Columbia University Press, 1968.

Sliger, Bernard F., Ansel M. Sharp, and Robert L. Sandmeyer. "Local Government Revenues: An Overview." In *Management Policies in Local Government Finance*, J. R. Aronson and Eli Schwarts, eds. Washington: International City Management Association, 1975, pp. 42–62.

Smith, Warren L. "Neo-Keynesian View of Monetary Policy." *Controlling Monetary Aggregates*. Federal Reserve Bank of Boston (June 1969), pp. 105–26.

Snyder, Louis L. *The Dynamics of Nationalism*. Princeton: Van Nostrand, 1964.

———. *Varieties of Nationalism: A Comparative Study*. Hinsdale, Ill.: Dryden Press, 1976.

Stein, Herbert. *Fiscal Revolution in America*. Chicago: University of Chicago Press, 1969.

Subcommittee on Foreign Economic Policy of the Joint Committee on Economic Report. Washington: U.S. Government Printing Office, 1955, pp. 453, 463.

Taylor, M. *Anarchy and Cooperation*. New York: Wiley, 1976.

Teigen, Ronald L. "A Critical Look at Monetarist Economics." *Review*. Federal Reserve Bank of St. Louis (January 1972), pp. 10–25.

Terpstra, Vern. *The Cultural Environment of International Business*. Cincinnati: South-Western, 1978, pp. 33–37, 56–57.

Tobin, James. "Friedman's Theoretical Framework." *Journal of Political Economy* (September-October 1972), pp. 852–63.

Tobin, James, and Willem Buiter. "Long-Run Effects of Fiscal and Monetary Policy on Aggregate Demand." Lowes Foundation Discussion Paper No. 384 (December 13, 1974).

Vedder, Richard, Lowell Gallaway, and Christopher Frenze. "Federal Tax Increases and Budget Deficit, 1947–86: Some Empirical Evidence." Joint Economic Committee Minority Staff Paper, 1987.

Wall Street Journal. "Creditor Nations Urged to Renew Debtor Reform." (April 24, 1989), p. B5B.

———. "Legislating Languages: Will It Work?" (March 13, 1973), p. 13.

World Bank. *Development Report*. Washington: World Bank, 1983.

Yeager, Leland B. *International Monetary Relations*. New York: Harper and Row, 1966.

Znaniecki, F. *Modern Nationalities: A Sociological Study*. Urbana: University of Illinois Press, 1952.

Index

ABOUT THE AUTHOR

GEORGE MACESICH is Professor of Economics and Director of the Center for Yugoslav-American Studies, Research, and Exchanges at Florida State University. In addition, he is an editorial consultant for several domestic and foreign professional journals, founding editor of *Proceedings and Reports*, and author of over twenty-five books including *Monetary Policy and Rational Expectations* (Praeger, 1987), *Monetary Reform and Cooperation Theory* (Praeger, 1989), and *Money and Democracy* (Praeger, 1990).